NO LOOKING BACK

Me and Yvette, 1970.

NO LOOKING BACK

ONE IRAQI JEWISH FAMILY'S FLIGHT TO FREEDOM

JOSEPH H. DABBY

SMALL
BATCH
BOOKS

493 SOUTH PLEASANT STREET
AMHERST, MASSACHUSETTS 01002
413.230.3943
SMALLBATCHBOOKS.COM

———— ❧ ————

To my parents, Naima and Haskel,
who gave me the map and compass of my life;
to my wife, Yvette, the love of my life
and my partner in this amazing journey;
and to my daughters, Naomi, Lisa, and Nadine,
who made it all worthwhile.

———— ❧ ————

Contents

The Revelation—Baghdad, 1956

I was ten when my eleven-year-old cousin Lydia turned to me and announced, "Your sister has just had a baby." We were sitting on the porch swing at my uncle's home on a cloudy winter afternoon.

"I don't have a sister." I looked at Lydia with a big smile. *What game is she playing with me this time?*

"Come on, Yousuf, of course you do. You have two sisters and a brother too."

"I have two sisters and a brother," I said sarcastically.

"Of course. Your brother's name is Saleh." Lydia rolled her eyes. "Why do you think everyone calls your dad Abu Saleh and not Abu Yousuf?" It is customary in Iraq to call men *Abu* (father of), followed by the name of their firstborn child.

"Stop it, Lydia. I have no siblings." *Now that's going too far.* I was getting angry.

"Yes, you do," Lydia asserted while twirling her short black hair. "They left for Israel when you were too young to remember."

That night during dinner, I asked my mother, "Mama, is it true that I have siblings?"

Mom bit her lip and looked at my father; for a moment she did not know what to say.

"Yes, *ibni* [my son], it's true," she said in a low voice.

"Why didn't you tell me?" I was upset.

"Your dad and I thought it would be better if you didn't know," Mom tried to explain.

"*Ibni*, we were afraid that you might talk about them and we would get in trouble," Dad said.

"How old are my siblings?" I asked, ignoring the excuses.

"Your brother, Saleh [Charles], is twelve years older than you." So, Lydia is right. That's why they call my father Abu Saleh.

"Your sisters, Berta and Tikva, are nine and seven years older than you," Mom said, putting her hand gently on mine. Sitting across the table from me, Dad watched my reactions as he leaned back in his seat and pushed his thin hair back with his hands.

"Why did you send them away?" I asked.

"We wanted a better life for them," Dad said.

"What do you mean?"

Mom and Dad looked at each other. "We wanted them to live where there is no discrimination, where no one would point at them because they are Jewish," Dad said.

"We sent them with their aunt to Israel." Mom wiped the tears running down her cheeks with her hand. "We were planning to join them a few weeks later, but it did not work out that way."

"What happened?" I was confused.

"One doesn't always get to do what one wants, *ibni*," Dad

said as he looked down at his hands resting on the table. "We would leave today if we could, but it is not so easy."

"The good thing is that you are spoiled as an only child." I knew that Mom was changing the subject. *If only she knew how I always longed to have siblings.*

I could not stop thinking how difficult it must have been for my parents to send their teenage children away. A decision like that is not easy to make. It was no secret that we had no future here—Mom and Dad talked about that all the time. We hardly interacted socially with non-Jews. All my friends from school were Jewish. We were taught to be passive and not to respond if confronted by a non-Jew. On the street we spoke in the Muslim dialect. We knew our place and limitations, and I always thought that was normal. That day I realized that our life was not normal, and that it was not if, but when, we would leave Iraq and join my siblings.

"Do you have photos of my siblings?" I asked Mom.

"Yes," she replied.

The old black-and-white photos were of another time. A portrait of my parents with my three siblings taken before I was born. A photo of Saleh and Berta standing with me in a baby carriage. School photos of my sisters with their classmates. Everyone seemed so happy.

"Let's write them a letter," Mom said. She brought out a pad and pen and put them in front of me. Neither Mom nor Dad could read or write. "Start by telling them we miss them," Mom directed me.

"*Ela Akhi wa akhwaty* [To my brother and sisters] . . ." I read back the words I wrote in Arabic. *Akhi wa akhwaty?* The words reverberated in my head. *Is this for real? I have a brother and two sisters?*

"The weather here has not been good recently," Mom dictated. "It has been very cloudy and windy, but no rain."

"Why are you telling them about the weather?" I asked.

"It's a code. It means that it has been difficult for us here, but everyone is okay," Mom explained. "We have packed but cannot move," Mom continued to dictate. "We are still looking for another house."

"What does that mean?"

"It means that Dad has wrapped up his business, but we cannot leave yet; we will continue trying," Mom said with tears in her eyes.

From then on I became the scribe, writing and reading the correspondence with my siblings. The letters were always written in code. "It is raining so hard, we have to stay home." *The situation is dire here, we are afraid to leave home.* "Your father cannot work anymore." *Your father's business license was canceled.* "Our phone is not working." *Our phone has been disconnected.*

I wrote letters to siblings I had never met and had no feelings for. There was no mail service between Israel and Iraq, so all the family correspondence was sent to a friend of the family in London, who replaced the envelopes and redirected the mail.

I was fifteen when I met my brother for the first time and twenty-six when I met my two sisters.

This is a story that unfolds somewhere in our world every day.

The story of those suffering discrimination and persecution, risking their lives to escape their country, leaving all they have behind, and hoping for a better life elsewhere.

The story of a community that was broken and fragmented, of families that were divided and scattered all over the world through no fault of their own, told by one of the fortunate few who survived.

The story of the ethnic cleansing of one of the oldest communities in the world—the Jews of Iraq—and the political turmoil in Iraq from 1940 to 1972.

This is my story.

CHAPTER 1

My Story Begins Before I Was Born

Naima sat on a wooden bench in the large courtyard of her home, sipping hot tea from a small glass. The coffee table in front of her was covered with plates full of *ba'ba'* and *sambousak* (cookies) that she had baked the day before for Shavuot (the holiday that commemorates the giving of the Torah to the Jewish people at Mount Sinai). She watched with pride her son and two young daughters playing together.

Where did the time go? she thought. *It's like yesterday that Saleh was born, and he is already seven, and Albertine and Esperance are four and two.*

Naima was very pleased with the beautiful dresses she had bought for herself and the girls for the holiday. Hers was a long, light-blue dress with long sleeves, adorned with tiny white flowers; Albertine's was red with a white collar; and Esperance's was bright yellow.

"I am hungry," Albertine whined, her siblings nodding in agreement.

Haskel and Naima and their children Saleh,
Albertine, and Esperance, circa 1944.

"Baba should be home any minute, and we will have a feast," Naima said. "Thank you children for helping me cook and prepare the table for dinner."

It was just before sunset, and the blue sky was turning red. The shadow of the balcony railings fell on the walls surrounding the courtyard like a painting. Naima looked at the open doors of the rooms that surrounded the courtyard and at the shining wet floor washed by the housekeeper earlier to cool the air. She remembered when Haskel showed her the house a few days after they got married. Unlike the other houses that lined the narrow and winding road, this house's *shanasheel* (overhanging bay

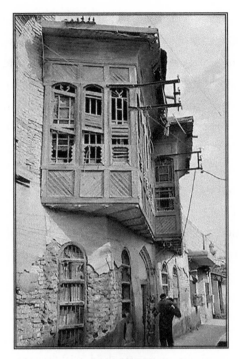

Shanasheel.

windows made of carved wood latticework) were colorful and amazing. The moment Naima walked through the front door, saw the airy and bright courtyard paved with brick laid in a basket-weave pattern, and looked up and saw the blue sky, she fell in love. She looked at Haskel and nodded. Haskel bought the house.

The door burst open, interrupting Naima's thoughts. Haskel rushed in, slammed the door closed, and started moving heavy pieces of furniture and leaning them against the door.

"Hagla [Haskel's nickname], what is going on? What are you doing?" Naima put her tea glass on the coffee table and walked toward him.

3

"Take the kids to the roof right now," Hagla answered in a distressed voice. "Mobs are pulling Jews out of busses and killing them. They are breaking into Jewish homes." He ran to the kitchen. "Don't just stand there, take the children and go to the roof."

Naima froze. She stood there watching Haskel in his suit and tie carry two cans of kerosene from the kitchen to the front door.

"What do you need that for?" she asked in panic.

"I will burn the house before anyone breaks in and hurts my family. Go to the roof," Haskel said as he wiped the sweat off his forehead. "Take the children and go to the roof."

Esperance started crying. Naima ran and grabbed the girls' hands and ran to the stairs. "Saleh, come with me," she said to him in a calm voice.

Naima and the three children went up the stairs to the roof. The beds were already set up and covered with mosquito netting. A clay water pitcher sat on the parapet with a silver bowl on top. Houses in the old city were attached, with short brick parapets separating their roofs. Naima saw their neighbor Abu Tabra, in his white dishdasha (ankle-length dress-like garb worn by men in the Middle East), spraying water on the floor of his roof to cool it down.

"*Massa'a al Kher* [Good evening], Naima, why is the child crying?" Abu Tabra asked.

Naima recounted what Haskel had told her.

"Call Abu Saleh to come up to the roof. I am going downstairs and won't let anyone get close to your door," Abu Tabra said as he turned the water off. "Don't worry."

Haskel would not come upstairs; he stayed next to the kerosene cans by the front door.

*Mobs attacking Jewish homes and institutions,
June 1–2, 1941.*

Naima could hear women screaming. She looked over the
parapet and saw smoke coming up from a house down the
street. She looked down, where Abu Tabra stood in the middle
of the narrow road with a big machete in his right hand, just in
time to stop an approaching mob of a few men holding sticks
and knives.

"Get out of the way," the man heading the group shouted as
he waved a thick stick in the air. "We are after the Jews, nothing
to do with you."

"Listen, my brother," Abu Tabra shouted back. "If you want
to go through, you have to kill me first." A couple of men came
out from their homes and stood behind Abu Tabra, backing him.
After a short, tense standoff, the attacking men turned around

and went away. Abu Tabra stood guard by the house all night, but Naima and Haskel did not sleep.

The Farhud ("dispossession" in Arabic), as it was later called, was a pogrom aimed at the Jewish community in Baghdad on June 1 and 2, 1941. It lasted forty-eight hours, during which 180 Jews were murdered and more than one thousand were injured. More than 800 Jewish homes were ransacked and destroyed, and many women were maimed and/or raped. It was a big wake-up call for the Jewish community, which until then had enjoyed relative security. During the British mandate (1919 to 1932), Jews were involved in every aspect of building the new country—they served as parliament members and ministers and helped develop the postal and railway services, and they were instrumental in creating the distinctive Iraqi music. In the years 1932 to 1941, Iraq was inundated by Nazi propaganda and anti-Semitic articles in local newspapers, pushed by the German embassy. New laws instituted in 1934, during the reign of King Ghazi, prohibited the teaching of the Hebrew language and established quotas for hiring Jews in civil service and for admitting Jewish kids to public schools. The Farhud was the last straw and the beginning of the end of normal life for the Jews. Iraq was no longer a safe country. Many left for India or other British colonies, and only a few of them returned when the dust settled down. But everyone knew that the day would soon come when all Jews would have to leave Iraq.

CHAPTER 2

Naima and Haskel

I was born to Naima and Haskel in the early morning of Monday, May 27, 1946. I was named Yousuf after my paternal grandfather, who had passed away one year before. By then, Naima and Haskel had three children—Saleh, twelve; Berta (Albertine), nine; and Tikva (Esperance), seven.

According to their Iraqi passports, Dad was born in 1899, and Mom was born in 1911. According to them, Dad was born in 1906 and Mom in 1910.

My grandfather Yousuf was married three times. He had no children from his first marriage. His second wife, Mass'ouda Shamash, bore him three boys—Elia, Khadouri, and Haskel, my dad. The eldest, Elia, married young and left home.

After the death of Mass'ouda, Grandfather Yousuf married Reema, who bore him two boys—Salman and Daoud—and a girl—Nazhima. Khadouri and Haskel were not happy with their stepmother and ran away from home to live with their brother Elia and his wife, Gurgiyi. Khadouri and Dad worked at a young age to support themselves and did not go to school.

Mom and me, 1947.

Me with Albertine and Saleh, 1947.

(Interesting sidenote: The four brothers—Khadouri, Haskel, Salman, and Daoud—each named a son Yousuf, after their father. Daoud's son Yousuf was one of the sixty-nine sailors who perished when the Israeli submarine *Dakar* sank mysteriously in the Mediterranean in 1968. Its remnants were found in 1999.)

In 1932 Dad was introduced to my mother, Naima Shemtov, and shortly thereafter, on December 7, 1932, they got married. Naima was the third of five children born to Saleh Shemtov and Chahla Is'hayek. Her father, Saleh, died young. Naima and her three sisters, Regina, Tova, and Salima, and her younger brother, Ezra, had to work from a young age to support the family.

In a photo taken around 1933, Dad appears slightly shorter than Mom, who was five-foot-eight. He was fair skinned, with green-hazel eyes and thinning black hair. Mom had black curly hair, brown eyes, and naturally tanned skin.

Naima and Haskel, 1933.

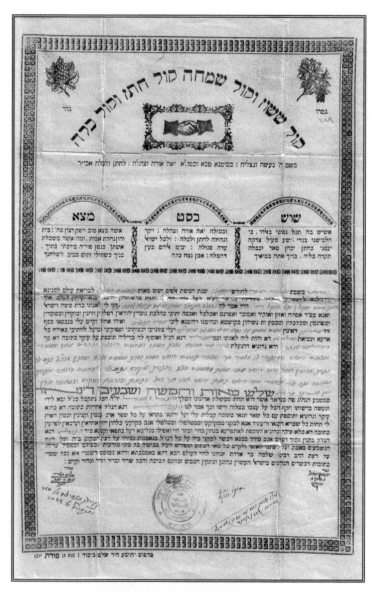

Naima and Haskel's ketubah,
written on December 7, 1932, in Baghdad.

Dad was a quiet man, easygoing but short-tempered. He had a heart of gold and would drop whatever he was doing to help others, friends or strangers. He was trusting, and that got him in trouble several times. He was known for his honesty and generosity. I remember going with him to visit Jewish prisoners, some of whom he did not even know. He prepared and took care packages to them and attended to their needs. The prisoners were grateful and called Dad their angel.

Dad was an importer and wholesaler of spices and herbs. He knew herbs so well that everyone thought of him as an herbalist. People swore by him and traveled long distances to seek his help in curing their ailments.

Mom was smart, wise, and strong-willed. Her lady friends always came to her for advice. She always knew what she wanted and went after it. She was always elegant. Her walk was assertive and confident. Appearance and posture were very important to her.

"Clothes make the person," Mom used to say. I was always in dress pants and dress shoes or sneakers. Mom did not allow me to wear khakis or sandals. She always reminded me to sit up straight and not to slouch. She taught me to fight for what I believe in, and to be organized.

"What will your wife say about me?" Mom would ask when she walked into my room and saw my clothes on the bed. "Always return what you use to its place; this way you always know where to find it when you need it."

I was very close to Mom, and it was much easier for me to go to her than to Dad when I got in trouble or needed something.

Mom and me, 1952.

Mom and Dad were always formal in their behavior and dress. I do not remember ever seeing Dad without a suit and a tie, even at picnics. Mom was always in dresses or suits. I never saw them holding hands or expressing their feelings to each other. I felt their love for me, but it was never conveyed by conversation or hugs. Dad treated me like an adult and wanted me to see his world and to learn. He emphasized hard and honest work and his belief in the goodness of people. My parents' actions and behavior, not their words, shaped my thinking, my morals, my beliefs, and my values.

A family picnic.

CHAPTER 3

Saleh

After the Farhud, Haskel decided to move the family away from downtown Baghdad. He felt that it would be safer for the family to live in a sparsely developed area where no one knew we were Jewish. He purchased a lot in Karrada, a new suburb south of Baghdad, and built a modern, two-story house in the middle of orange groves. I was two years old when we moved into our new home.

Trouble followed anyway. What Haskel did not know was that his son Saleh was involved in the Zionist movement and was holding regular meetings with his group in the basement of our new home. The group studied Hebrew, learned how to use a gun, and talked about emigrating to the promised land—Israel.

When Israel declared its statehood in May 1948, the Iraqi government considered every Jew either a Zionist, a Communist, or both. Many were imprisoned and subjected to mock trials, and some were hanged in public. The hanging of Shafiq Ades, a rich Jewish businessman in Basra, in front of his home

Saleh, 1953.

on September 23, 1948, shocked the whole country. He was accused both of helping Israel and being a Communist. Nothing could help him, not even his close friendship with the regent and the royal family. The message to all Iraqis was that no one is untouchable. The murder of Ades reinforced the desire of the Jews to leave Iraq.

On a summer day in 1950, Haskel came home from work unexpectedly, around noon. He came in a taxi, which was unusual; moreover, he had the taxi wait in front of the house.

"Where is Saleh?" he asked Naima as he walked hurriedly by her.

"In his room." She turned around and followed him.

Haskel ran upstairs to Saleh's room. "Saleh, pack some

clothes, and let's go," he told his bewildered son, who was sitting at his desk studying.

"What's going on, Dad?" Saleh asked.

"They are coming to get you any minute," Haskel retorted. "Pack some clothes in a duffel bag, now."

"Hagla, what is happening? Tell me." Naima stood at the door, scared and anxious. She had never seen Haskel so nervous.

"The Mukhabarat [intelligence service] will be here any minute. They are looking for Saleh," Haskel said.

"Why, what did he do?" Naima asked with her hands over her mouth.

"Dhafer called me an hour ago." Dhafer, a member of the secret police, was a friend of the family. "Dhafer said that Saleh's name came up on a list of Zionists, and he advised me to get him out of the country as soon as possible," Haskel said.

Naima started crying, while Saleh dropped everything, grabbed some clothes, and shoved them in his duffel bag. "They took Jamil this morning," he said in a low voice. Jamil was Saleh's closest friend.

"Where are you taking him?" Naima asked Haskel.

"He is going to Basra, where his uncle can have him smuggled out of the country."

Naima was speechless. It was not real. It felt like she was watching a movie.

Haskel and Saleh ran down the stairs and got in the taxi. Naima stood at the front door of the house, crying, not knowing if she would ever see Saleh again. She did not even have a chance to hug or kiss him goodbye. "I didn't even see what he packed," she mumbled under her breath. "I hope he took warm clothes."

The taxi took Haskel and Saleh to the train station, where Saleh took the overnight train to Basra to join his uncle Khadouri, who lived there at the time.

After a few days in Basra, Khadouri arranged for a smuggler to take Saleh across Shatt al-Arab River to Iran. Saleh made the trip to Abadan, a small port town in Iran, on a fisherman's boat. He was hidden under fishing nets and canvas in a corner of the boat. From Abadan, Saleh traveled to Tehran, where he stayed a few days with friends of Dad, and then flew to Istanbul, where he was supposed to stay and finish high school. However, Saleh had other plans—he followed his dream and migrated to Israel. He was sixteen.

CHAPTER 4
Berta and Tikva

From 1948 to 1950 it was a time of fear and uncertainty for the Jews in Iraq. Life was getting more difficult every day as the government made new laws restricting their movements and activities. The Jews started to look for ways to leave the country, and many escaped to Iran.

To stop the uncontrollable emigration of Jews and their assets, in March 1950 the Iraqi government, under Prime Minister Tawfiq al-Suwaidi, issued an amendment to Law 1, the Denaturalization Act. This amendment was taken from the Nazi policy book. It allowed Jews to leave the country with one caveat—their citizenship would be revoked. The government thought that only 7,000 to 10,000 of the 150,000 Iraqi Jews at the time would opt to leave the country.

Initially very few people applied for exit visas. Most feared the unknown and preferred to stay put with the devil they knew. Then bombs exploded in a synagogue and in a coffee shop frequented by the Jews. The Jewish community was terrified. To the

Our family in Baghdad, 1950.

surprise of the government, within a few days, around 120,000 Jews applied for passports and exit visas. This was later known as the Big Aliyah.

Many people think that Israel was behind the bombing to scare the Jews into emigrating. It was also rumored that Iraq was paid by the British to let the Jews leave and to take in the Palestinian refugees instead, housing them in a town south of Baghdad, to be built by England with American money.

All of our extended family registered to leave the country. Haskel and Naima decided to send their two teenage daughters,

Berta, then fourteen, and Tikva, twelve, with their aunt Tova to Israel, planning to follow them.

"Your father and I will be with you soon," Mom assured the two girls at the airport, but her comforting words did not stop them from crying.

"Don't lose your stuffed toys; I sewed gold coins into them," she whispered in their ears. They hung on to her hand as they were being pulled by their aunt. My parents watched with tears in their eyes as their young daughters were herded like sheep into planes without seats. Everyone's luggage and whatever they carried was taken from them by the authorities before they boarded the planes, but the young girls got to keep their stuffed toys.

I was five years old when my sisters left for Israel in May 1952 with my aunt.

Dad started to liquidate his assets in order to leave the country and join my siblings. He sold his dream house in 1952, and we moved into a rented *mushtamal* (small cottage) a few blocks away. Most of our furniture was given away, as only so much furniture could fit in the *mushtamal*.

Mom and I were the last ones to leave the big empty house. We walked the few blocks to the *mushtamal*. My dog, Rex, a white cairn terrier, followed us, running a couple of feet behind me. Rex and I were inseparable. I played with him and confided in him. We even dug holes together. What saddens me is that I do not remember where he came from or what happened to him.

We had only been in the new place a few months when trouble came to us unexpectedly. Dad did not come back from work one day. Mom called Dad's business partner, who told her that Dad left the *makhzan* (store) with two men whom he believed

With my father and Rex, my dog.

were from the Amn (national security). In the morning, Mom put on her abaya (a loose black cloak Muslim women wear on top of their clothes), covered her hair with a black scarf, and left to look for Dad. She did not come home till dark, but Dad was not with her. Day after day, she kept looking. She never gave up. She reached out to every influential person she knew, hoping to find out where Dad was being held—without success. Dad had just vanished.

Around noon on the fifth day, Dad showed up. He was disheveled and had a long beard. He told us that he had been taken by the Amn and was held at their headquarters, where he was interrogated.

"They hit me on my back and legs with a rubber hose and wanted me to confess to being a spy." Dad told us that he was taken because he had seen off a Syrian business associate at the airport. He was told that the Syrian was a spy. "I thought I would not leave my cell alive. This morning, without any explanation, they released me."

"Thank God," Mom said, looking at the ceiling.

"But now I have to report to the police every two weeks until their investigation is completed. We won't be able to leave the country for some time now," Dad told Mom.

Mom didn't say anything, just bit her lower lip as she always did when things did not go well. With that, my parents' plan to join their children was put on hold and did not materialize for another twenty years.

Now it was final: Our family had split into two.

Family of three.

Chapter 5

Moving Again

In the spring, when the snow on top of the mountains in Turkey and northern Iraq melted, the Dejla River (Tigris) swelled and sometimes flooded Baghdad. The flood of March 1954 was one of the worst that Baghdad had seen. Our suburb of Karadah was under water and was evacuated. We moved in with family for a few days.

We headed home when the evacuation was removed. It was dusk as the cab turned onto our street. Both sides of the narrow, stone-paved road were muddy puddles of water. Sitting in the front passenger seat, my father, with his disheveled, thinning hair, said, "Glad we are going back, the water is practically gone."

"I am so scared to go into the house. I don't know what to expect," Mom muttered. I could feel her hand tremble as she sat next to me in the back of the car.

The car stopped and the three of us got out. My father folded his pants up and started hopping from stone to stone, not stepping in the mud, toward the front gate. His jacket and tie swayed from side to side.

The flood of 1954.

Mom took off her shoes and followed my dad, gracefully stepping on the same stones. She stood by the door and turned toward me. "Come now, you can do it," she said. "Be careful not to step in the mud."

When Dad opened the front door of the *mushtamal*, water rushed out. *There goes our effort to stay dry*, I thought. My father was the first to wade in. Mom hesitated, then she let go of my hand and said, "You stay here." I could see beyond the vestibule the red Persian carpet covered with three inches of dirty water. At that moment all I could think about was the truck and bike I had erected with my Meccano set. *They must be covered with water and rusted by now.* Dad came back holding a shovel and a broom.

"Walk behind me and push the water out," he said as he handed my mom the broom. Without saying a word, my mom took the broom and followed him.

It took days for the carpets and floors to dry, and our living room furniture was so damaged that it had to be thrown out.

"I saw a house for rent two blocks away," Dad announced a few days later. "It's one stair flight above the street and was not flooded. I talked to the owner and we can move there next week." Mom nodded her head; she thought it was a good idea. We moved again.

Across the street from our new house lived a Kurdish family. I became friends with their children and spent a lot of time playing with them. Omid, the oldest son, taught me to play the harmonica. Serwan, who was a couple of years older than me, and I spent hours standing across the street from each other, each at his front gate, communicating with paper cup "telephones" connected by a string, which we let loose when cars passed by. We loved cars and airplanes. We accumulated a list of more than fifty pages of all the cars that drove on our street: make, model, color, and license plate. We bought and collected small British books that were published annually with pictures and specifications of new civilian and military planes. We also cruised the area on our bikes.

A few years later, we moved again, this time to a newer house in the same area. I saw less and less of Serwan and Omid. Sixty years later, I found Serwan on Facebook. He was still in Baghdad. It was wonderful to talk to him on the phone after so long.

When television came to Baghdad in 1956, Dad bought a set and plugged it in in the living room. Guests and friends came to our house to see the new marvel. It was winter, and they sat around the *sopa* and watched with amazement. The *sopa*, an Aladdin blue-flame kerosene heater, was lit and placed in the middle of the living or family room with a kettle full of water on top. It was the house heater. The steam from the boiling water humidified the house. In addition, the *sopa* was used to brew tea and to roast chestnuts.

To cool the house during the hot Baghdad summer, one window in every room was covered with thorn plants placed between two pieces of wood lattice and kept wet by water dripping from a hose to cool the air flowing through the window.

By the sixties, television and radio became the mouthpieces of the regime. It was rumored during the Ba'ath regime that television broadcasts were used to convey messages to the Ba'ath party members. When the video of a certain belly dancer interrupted the regular television program, it signaled a call to members of the party, so people stopped what they were doing and rushed to their homes, fearing the worst.

Sopa.

CHAPTER 6

Stories From My Childhood

The Souk

Shopping for groceries with Dad is one of the many memories I treasure.

Dad woke me up before sunrise. "Yousuf, Yousuf, wake up. It's time to go to the souk."

I opened my eyes. Dad was standing by my bed, gently shaking my shoulder with his left hand. He slipped a T-shirt on me and helped me with my shorts, socks, and sneakers. It was still dark, but I did not mind. I loved going to the souk, where the vendors were nice to me and always gave me samples.

We felt the cool breeze as we walked up our unpaved street to the main road. Dad held my hand with his left hand and carried an empty *zanbeel* (a sack woven of palm tree fronds) in his right hand. We waited for the bus at the main road, and when it appeared in the distance, my father stepped into the road and signaled for it to stop.

Private buses were the only transportation method in new areas of the city. These were small wood-cabin buses that seated ten people. A teenage boy sat on the step to the bus and held the door halfway open. He let the passengers on and off and collected the fares. We got on the rickety bus, and Dad paid the boy twenty *fils*, the fare for two, the equivalent of six U.S. cents at the time. The trip to the souk in downtown Baghdad took about thirty minutes.

Souk Hanoon, a narrow, unpaved pathway covered with tarps for protection from the elements, was saturated with the strong smell of meats and fruits and the deafening noise of vendors and shoppers bargaining. Occasionally the screams of a Kurdish porter carrying a heavy sack on his back asking people to make way pierced the air. Vendors sat on the ground on each side of the pathway, shouting the great bargains they were offering. Walking down the pathway, Dad checked out the merchandise. Then he stopped and bent to pick up a cucumber.

"How much?" he asked.

"Twenty *fils* a kilo," the woman in black garb answered.

"Thirty *fils* for two kilos." Bargaining was a normal ritual. "Bargaining is good," Dad used to say, "as long as you leave something for the other guy." My bargaining skills came from watching my dad at the *makhzan* and at the souk.

"Thirty-five *fils*, final," the vendor said and handed me a cucumber to eat.

Dad bent down, picked the cucumbers he liked, and placed them on the scale. He paid the woman, then threw the cucumbers in his *zanbeel*. Dad moved between the vendors, picking up squash, tomatoes, lettuce, grapes, apples, etc. After haggling over the price at every stop, coins exchanged hands, and more vegetables and fruits were thrown into the *zanbeel*. We walked back to the road, Dad leaning to his right under the weight of the heavy *zanbeel*. My shorts were almost falling to the ground from the weight of fruit samples that filled my pockets.

For the meats we went to a different souk at Bistan Al Khas (the lettuce orchard), in the suburb of Bataween. We got lamb, the preferred red meat in Iraq, from the Jewish butcher's store. Outside the butcher's store, next to cages full of live chickens, stood the *shohet* (Hebrew for the man who slaughters chickens). My father pointed to the chicken he liked, the *shohet* took the unlucky chicken out, slit its throat, and dumped it in a barrel, where it bounced uncontrollably against the barrel's walls for a few minutes, then took it inside the store for the butcher to clean.

Learning to Swim in the Dejla (Tigris River)

Mom was the enforcer. She was the one who decided what I could wear, what school I went to, and what extracurricular activities I should be involved in. When I turned five, Mom decided it was time for me to learn to swim. She took me by bus five days a week to a *chardagh* (a hut built of woven, dried palm tree fronds) on the edge of the Dejla, which was used as a swimming school. We had to take a thirty-minute bus ride to Bataween, walk about one mile to Abu Nawas Street, which ran parallel to the river, then walk down the hill to the *chardagh*.

The *chardagh* was run by two *sabbahs* (swimming teachers)— Hai, who was Jewish, blond, and physically fit, and Ali, a dark-skinned and heavyset Muslim. The kids were fitted with *karab* (floats made from the dried end of palm fronds tied together with a piece of rope). Beginners started with three *karab,* one on their chest and the other two on their back. The number of *karab* went down as the kids learned to swim, until they no longer needed them. We used to fight for the smaller *karba* (singular of *karab*) because it was light and not as restraining as the large ones.

The *sabbah* swam inside an inner tube of a truck tire and led the group of kids of different ages to one of the small islands that appeared in the middle of the Dejla every summer. To motivate and encourage us, the *sabbah* chanted a song about a famous Jewish swimmer called Balboul (a play on the word *bulbul,* Arabic for "nightingale"). We responded with "*bali*" (yes) at the end of every verse. The song went like this: "*Bali, ya awlad Balboul, bali, ma sheft al asfour, bali, yengur bil tassa, bali, haleeb ib rassa, bali.*" ("Yes, children of Balboul, yes, did you see the bird, yes, picking at the bowl, yes, splashing milk on its head, yes.")

The water current in the Dejla was very strong and took the swimmers down the river, far away from the *chardagh.* We had to walk up the river on the sandy island beyond the location of the *chardagh* before we swam back. Advanced groups would swim across the river and back.

Loose Tooth

Dad had fun playing with me. I had a loose milk tooth, and Dad made no qualms about his desire to pull it out. I was very scared and tried to stay away from him for days.

"Let's do it," Dad said one day as he got up from his chair.

"No, Dad, please don't!"

I ran out to the garden, which was more of a grove than a garden, divided in square-shaped sections by small irrigation channels. I zigzagged between the fruit trees, jumping over watering channels and flower beds. Dad ran behind me, and finally he caught me. He put his finger in my mouth. He barely touched the shaky tooth before it fell in his palm. I was terrified but felt no pain. My father laughed, then he gave me the tooth and hugged me. "I will take you tomorrow to Mr. Shohet's office," he promised. Mr. Shohet, a toy broker, always had the latest toys in his office, and Dad knew that I loved going there.

The next day, Dad and I climbed up the steep flight of stairs to Mr. Shohet's office. You can only imagine my excitement, as this was where I got toys that were not on the market yet. Every toy Mr. Shohet gave me was a pleasant surprise.

When he saw us, Mr. Shohet got up from behind his desk. "Yousuf, let's see what we have for you today." He opened a small closet, got up on a stepladder, then pulled a box from the top shelf. He held the box in his hands and looked at it for a few long minutes before looking at me.

"This just came in from London. I think you'll love it."

It was a red bus with a removable transparent top and passengers in sitting and standing positions. It became my favorite toy; I spent hours placing passengers in different seats and moving the bus from station to station around the living room.

My Love for Music

Mom taught me to love music and the arts. She took me to the theater regularly to watch plays and concerts. Going to the theater, where the dress was formal and the spectators were appreciative of those on the stage, was a wonderful experience. It was like going to a different world and a different era.

When I turned nine, Mom decided I should learn to play a musical instrument. I chose the violin. It never occurred to me that maybe not everyone in the house would be happy about this. When I got my new violin, I took it out of the box with awe. It was the beautiful reddish-brown instrument that I had been dreaming of. I pulled the bow over the strings, pretending to play music. Dad must have heard the few notes, because he ran down the stairs. His rushed steps sounded heavy and frightening. Dad had just come home from work and his white shirt was half unbuttoned.

"Give me that!" he said angrily, pointing at the violin.

Mom came running after him, pleading, "Stop, Abu Saleh, stop, please." She always called him Abu Saleh (the father of Saleh) and not Hagla when she wanted something. "Please, Abu Saleh, let him be."

Dad took the violin from my hands. "My son will not play the violin." He turned to my mom. "Does he need black sunglasses too?"

"Abu Saleh, not all violin players are blind. Yousuf loves music and loves the sound of the violin. The music tutor will be here in one hour, please. . . ." She stopped. It was useless.

"I told you to buy him an accordion, not a violin," said Dad.

"But Baba, I don't like the accordion . . . ," I remember saying.

"If you want to learn to play a musical instrument, it will be the accordion," he said, then turned toward Mom. "Take this back and exchange it for an accordion." He handed her the violin and walked away.

I sat with the bow still in my hand. Mom stood there helpless, leaning against the door frame, holding the violin with both hands.

"Your dad does not want his son to play the violin. He thinks only the blind learn to play it to have a career as a musician." She came closer and sat on the chair next to me. Her prescription glasses were fogged up. "The accordion is a beautiful instrument, my darling. Learn to play music and you can get a violin later, your dad will change his mind. . . ."

"No, no . . . I hate the accordion. I do not want an accordion." Tears were running down my cheeks. Mom wiped my tears with the small white lace hankie she always had on her.

"It's okay, Yousuf. I promise to get you a violin later. . . . We have to do what Dad says now."

WHY? I asked myself. *Why can't Baba listen to me once? It is always "Baba wants this, Baba wants that. . . ."* I hugged Mom. Placing the violin back in its box, she put her arms around me. She was always gentle, soft-spoken, and calming.

A few days later Mom got me a beautiful red accordion. "Sit down and let's try it," she said. She slipped the shoulder straps over my arms and placed the accordion on my lap. It was heavy. I held the keyboard with my right hand and pulled the accordion open as I pressed a key. A loud note shook the room, and I almost lost my balance.

With a big smile, Mom said, "See? You can do it. I am so proud of you."

I do not remember ever holding that accordion again, nor did I get to learn music, which I truly regret.

Amba (Pickled Mango)

Dad took the bus every morning, six days a week, to his *makhzan* in the Shorja bazaar, about forty minutes from home, and came back home around 4:00 p.m. His worker would come to our house to pick up a freshly cooked lunch for him at midday. After dinner, at around 6:00 p.m., Dad would take the bus to Gahwat Hassan (Hassan's Café) in Bataween, a twenty-minute bus ride. He took me with him most of the time. At the café, men sat outdoors in the summer and crowded into a steamy room in the winter. They chatted, drank tea or Arabic coffee, smoked the *nargila* (hookah), and played backgammon or dominoes. Snacks of fava beans and za'atar or long green beans were served. In the meantime, I ran around and played with other kids. By 9:00 p.m. we would be back home.

One summer evening Dad surprised me. "Tomorrow you are coming with me to learn how to mix *amba* [pickled mango slices]." Dad was one of the biggest importers of *amba*, a very popular condiment, in Iraq. It has a special taste—one either likes it or hates it.

"But tomorrow is Friday and everything is closed," Mom reminded Dad.

"That's why we are going tomorrow. I don't want anyone to learn my secret recipe." Dad smiled, looking at me. "But first we have to bathe. Let's go, Yousuf."

We had no running hot water in those days. A big pot full of hot water was brought from the kitchen and mixed with cold water from the faucet in a big bowl. The concrete bathroom floor was too warm for my bare feet—it was heated by burning wood underneath.

Dad rubbed his body with a gray powder. "This is called *dawa hamam* [bath medicine]. I use it to remove my body hair to make sure the spices I mix are always clean," Dad explained. He scrubbed my body with soap and a flat loofah and washed me down with a silver goblet before he washed the *dawa hamam* off his body and bathed himself.

The Shorja bazaar felt strange on Fridays, the weekly day off in Iraq. All the shops were closed, and very few people walked around. On a regular business day, the bazaar would be crowded with shoppers moving very slowly, checking every store. The bazaar was an unpaved wide passage covered with tarp, with small stores on both sides that sold everything imaginable: food, clothing, stationery, etc. There were also specialty sections in the bazaar where all the stores sold only dried fruits and nuts, or only toys, or only sweets.

Dad's *makhzan* was in a narrow alley off the bazaar, next to a small coffee shop frequented by Kurdish porters. These big and strong men were essential to the shops. On their padded backs they could carry heavy burlap bags or barrels weighing as much as two hundred kilos each, from trucks on the main road to the *makhzans* or between *makhzans*.

Dad unlocked the door of the *makhzan* and we went down the short flight of stairs to the main area, part of which was used as the office. Large rooms surrounded the office area and were filled with boxes and burlap bags of spices imported from faraway lands. The strong spice scent permeated the *makhzan* and the whole alley.

On weekdays the *makhzan* was a busy place. Retailers would come by to sample the spices and place their orders. Kurdish porters would be bringing in or taking out heavy burlap bags. When clients came in, there was social chatter and loud laughs followed by intense bargaining. During my summer vacation my father would take me with him to work. Azouri (his partner Naeem's son) and I played and ran up and down in the *makhzan* all day.

Dad moved a heavy barrel of *amba* to the middle of the *makhzan* and opened it. On a table not far from the barrel, he set up a few bottles of vinegar and bags of all kinds of spices. He proceeded to take off all his clothes except for his underpants and stood in front of the barrel.

"Yousuf, hand me the two small bottles and the spice bags on the table."

He poured the vinegar out of the two bottles into the barrel and added some of the spices. As he stirred the barrel's contents with a long wooden spoon, he looked at me and said, "Watch closely *ibni*, I want you to learn."

I was captivated watching Dad so engulfed in his work, bent over the barrel mixing the concoction. The sunrays were hitting his sweat-covered, half-naked body. He used no measuring tool to control the mix, just a splash of this, a handful of that, and so on. I could see his pride in his work. When done stirring the mixture, he brought in baby barrels and filled them with the new and improved *amba*. It took a long time to fill up and seal the small barrels. Finally, with beads of sweat running down his forehead, he stood back and looked at me. He filled a small cup and handed it to me.

"Here, *ibni*, try this," Dad said. Unlike the sour-tasting *amba* in pita bread we lined up to buy for lunch from Abu Kadhem at the school snack shop, Dad's *amba* was delicious—a bit vinegary and mildly spiced.

"By Monday afternoon all these small barrels will be gone; the fast-food shops on Rasheed Street cannot get enough of them," Dad said proudly. "Remember, *ibni*: To guarantee the best result, you have to do it yourself."

That advice stuck with me. To this day, I prefer to do the work myself, and in a way that may have been a hinderance to my business growth in certain instances.

Family Outings

On summer nights, once a week, my uncle's family, the Iny family, and our family would rent rowboats with rowers, bring on board all picnic supplies, food, and fruits, and navigate together to one of the small islands in the middle of the Dejla. There the kids would swim, and the adults would eat, drink, and listen to music. Watermelons were left to float in the water to keep them cool. It was a party, six adults and twelve kids talking, shouting, and singing while eating and drinking.

The Inys owned a big farm in the Diyala province, on the outskirts of Baghdad. Most of our Saturdays were spent with them and my uncle's family on their farm. The kids ran around while the adults socialized and played backgammon or cards. There was always lots of food. My cousins Farah (Kathy) and Eva Iny and I would get on top of the truck cabin and into the basket above its cockpit. We would sit in the basket singing as the truck traveled around the farm collecting oranges, lemons, and other fruits. Our parents thought that was okay!

Cruising

Mom always dragged me along with her on outings and visits with her friends. Going on car rides with Mom and her friend Mrs. Kahtan may have been the reason I grew up loving cars. On hot summer afternoons, Mrs. Kahtan invited us to join her for a ride around the city in her chauffeured 1940 Chevy. The rear door of the car was hinged at the back and opened to the front. These doors were called "suicide doors" at the time because they were less safe than doors hinged at the front. Mrs. Kahtan held the rear door of the car open while the car moved to let the air in to keep us cool. Her short gray hair would fly into her face as the wind blew around her. She was heavyset and always wore wide and long dresses. I can still feel Mom's arm around me to keep me from falling out of the car. Those were unforgettable moments when I felt her love.

At the time, there were no traffic signs in Baghdad. To slow down the traffic, huge, well-landscaped traffic circles and round-abouts were placed at every major intersection. At the center was a flower garden or a large water fountain where the lighting changed the color of the sprayed water. This was surrounded by a wide, grassy path bordered by a solid hedge on the street side. After sunset the temperature cooled down and people flocked to these roundabouts to sit on the benches along the path or walk around the circle.

Mrs. Kahtan always brought along Coca-Cola bottles in

a portable cooler, and Mom brought nuts and cookies. They walked around the circle while I ran and played with other kids. Wearing shorts, my knees got green and itchy from sliding on the grass. Mom always complained and gave me a bath after each of these outings.

World Affairs

My love of foreign affairs and world news came from my dad. I sat next to him every evening to listen to the news broadcasts from the BBC or VOA (Voice of America).

"If you are not aware of what is happening in our world," he used to tell me, "your life is not complete."

I was spending the day with Dad at his *makhzan* when a man stuck his head in the doorway and shouted, "Demonstration on Rasheed Street, close the shop!"

Immediately, Dad stopped what he was doing and turned the lights off.

"Yousuf, let's go."

Demonstrations were illegal, except for those organized by the government against Israel and America, and it was neither wise nor safe to be caught close to one. Dad locked the shop, grabbed my hand, and we ran to the main street, where we saw people four rows deep watching the demonstrations.

"We should not be here," Dad said, "but I want you to see." He lifted me up and seated me on his shoulders. Hundreds of people walked, carrying big banners, burning flags, and screaming, "Death to Israel, death to the Jews." The demonstration was to protest the 1956 war waged by the British, French, and Israelis against Egypt. In July 1956 Egyptian President Gamal Abdel Nasser nationalized the Suez Canal, which was owned and run by the British and the French. The nationalization threatened the transportation of oil to Europe. In late October of 1956, Britain, France, and Israel attacked Egypt, pushed through the Sinai Desert, and gained control of the canal, which caused lots of turmoil in the Middle East.

This was the first demonstration I ever saw. I saw the hate for us that people around us harbored come to the surface. I was afraid and started trembling. Dad brought me down from his shoulders and hugged me.

"Don't be scared, *ibni*," he said. "*Inshallah* [By God's will] they keep busy demonstrating and forget about us."

My First Cigarette

I got my first cigarette when I was ten from Rukun, our house-keeper, in exchange for ten *fils* (a dime). Rukun was an older *shurgawia* (woman who lived in a mud hut) from a poor neigh-borhood on the outskirts of Baghdad. Her skin was tanned dark from the sun, and wrinkles dominated her face. She was always dressed in black, with a black scarf wrapped around her head to cover her hair. On the street she would wear an abaya. She commuted to our house six days a week and did the cleaning, the laundry, and the dishes. My first cigarette was unfiltered and strong, and the first puff triggered a prolonged and stubborn cough. Rukun ran to bring me a glass of water. When she came back, she could not help but smile; I was inhaling like a pro. I can still feel the bitter taste of that cigarette on my tongue.

Shabbat (Saturday)

Every Shabbat, Dad woke me up at dawn to accompany him to the synagogue, and every time I begged him to let me sleep more. "*Rasha* [Nonobservant], get up," he would say as he pulled me off the bed.

Meals on Shabbat were special. Breakfast and lunch were prepared on Friday and cooked overnight because we did not use electricity or fire on Shabbat. On Friday Mom prepared *t'beet*, a traditional Iraqi Jewish dish for Shabbat, which took time to prepare and cook. A whole chicken would be stuffed with rice and spices and sewn closed, then it was placed on a bed of rice, tomato sauce, and spices and cooked slowly overnight on a kerosene stove. On top of the *t'beet* pot sat a smaller pot with eggs. The slow-cooked eggs became brown. For breakfast we had the brown eggs with fried eggplant slices, salads, parsley, and *amba* in a *laffa*, or pita bread. Today this sandwich is called *sabih*, named after the Iraqi man who brought it to Israel. At noon the *t'beet* was the meal everyone waited for, even the neighbor lady who was called to turn the fire off.

The Holy Days

The Jewish community was traditional in its religious observance; there were no denominations. The High Holy Days brought the community together and offered a distraction and respite from reality. Most of the community attended services at the synagogues and exchanged visits.

For Shavuot, Mom prepared the *kahi* (puff pastry), which

was baked at the local bakery. *Kahi* was usually served with *qaymar* (fresh cream), a popular breakfast dish in Iraq made from milk of the *jamoos* (water buffalo). *Qaymar* is dense, about three quarters of an inch thick, and is served with bread and *silan* (date syrup).

Early in the morning on the first day of Shavuot, I biked to the market, only a few blocks from our home, to buy the *qaymar* from one of the many Arab women who sat on the ground in front of large metal trays with *qaymar* covered with netting to protect it from flies. The women, all dressed in black with black hijabs and abayas, used a pin to cut a triangle of *qaymar* and put it on the buyer's plate using a spatula.

At Shavuot it was customary to visit the tomb of the prophet Ezekiel in Al Kifl, a village about ninety miles southwest of Baghdad. In 597 BCE, Ezekiel was brought as a slave from Jerusalem to Babylon, where he died in 569 BCE. Families traveled in caravans of private cars and taxis to visit his shrine. Typically, we joined Uncle Khadouri's family and the Iny family. On the way there, we stopped at a café in Al Mahmoudia, by the Euphrates River, for tea and *qaymar*.

At Al Kifl we walked through the souk to the shrine. Entering the shrine, we walked by several alcoves, each housing a prophet's grave. Ezekiel's grave sat by itself in the center of a large room and was enclosed by a large wooden box wrapped in blue velvet. The ceiling and the walls of the room were covered with golden and silver Hebrew letters and symbols. We would walk around Ezekiel's grave singing Hebrew songs from the Torah.

In the corner of the room, there was a big stone that everyone believed healed ailments, so people took turns holding it and passing it over their bodies. The stone was very smooth, probably as a result of its use over the years.

On the way back home, we stopped along the road to have a late lunch. Every family brought out the food they had prepared: rice, chicken stews, fruits, and vegetables, which we all shared.

One memory that sticks in my mind is stopping by the romaine lettuce fields on the way back home. We bought heads of lettuce from farmers who stood by the side of the road. The farmers washed the lettuce by dipping it in buckets filled with muddy water from the irrigation channels. We ate the lettuce one leaf at a time while watching septic tank trucks in the distance dumping raw sewage onto the rows of lettuce plants as fertilizer.

Two Scares

Twice during my childhood I was scared of losing a parent.

When I was eight, Dad had a stroke. We were at a party, and he was sitting with a group of men, chatting and smoking. Suddenly the cigarette fell out of his hand, he collapsed, and his body leaned sideways. Luckily, a doctor among the guests managed to revive him before the ambulance arrived. I was so scared as he lay on the couch. *Oh my God,* I thought, *Dad is dying. Who is going to take care of us?* Luckily, Dad recovered and stopped smoking.

When I was eleven, Mom had to go to the women's hospital, where she was scheduled for an outpatient procedure. She took me along because she did not want to leave me home alone.

"You sit on this bench and wait for me," she told me before going into the hospital. The bench was at a bus station at the entrance to the hospital. I sat there waiting. Buses came and left, people got on and off. To pass the time I counted the red cars passing by, then the green cars. As it was getting dark, I started thinking, *What if something goes wrong? What if Mom does not come out from the hospital? Who will take me home? What will I do without Mom?* I started crying.

Suddenly, I heard Mom's voice. I turned around, and she waved to me from the door of the hospital. She started walking slowly toward me. I could not wait, and I ran across the driveway and hugged her. She bent down to kiss my head.

"Don't leave me again, please," I said as she wiped the tears off my cheeks.

Today, thirty years after Mom passed, I still think she will open the door for me when I come home at the end of the day.

CHAPTER 7

Paralysis and Revolution, 1958

I was ten when I found out I had a brother and two sisters, all older than me, who lived far away, where we could not contact them directly. I wanted to know why they sent them away, why we did not join them after all these years, why no one bothered to tell me. . . . There was no end to my questions. I could not imagine what my parents felt living away from their children, and how my siblings, teenagers at the time, managed on their own.

My parents were reluctant to talk about it. Mom cried every time I broached the subject. I was too young to understand the complexities of the political situation. I understood, though, that my parents wanted a better life for all of us, and they sent their children ahead, planning to join them within a short time. I also understood that the situation changed and it was not possible for my parents to follow their children.

As the time passed, and as my siblings got older, Dad decided he was too old and would not consider leaving Iraq anymore.

"I would rather die here than be dependent on others," he would say. Mom agreed with him. "We are illiterate, and at our age to learn and to change is impossible," she would say. "I would rather stay here."

Like my parents, I accepted reality. We were here, they were there, and maybe one day we would meet. A sad conclusion.

In the summer of 1958, when Mom was about forty-eight, without any notice, she became paralyzed from the waist down and lost sensation in her lower body. Many doctors were consulted, but no one knew the cause or could prescribe a medication. Physical therapy did not help. A doctor recommended heat by steam, but that burned Mom's legs and thighs because she couldn't feel the heat. In June my parents got permission from the government to travel to London for treatment, on the condition that I stayed behind to ensure their return. I stayed with Uncle Khadouri's family.

Dad and his brother Khadouri were very close, and so were our two families.

Mom introduced Uncle Khadouri to Simha in 1942, after his first wife, Naima, passed. They got married and had three girls—Naomi, Lydia, and Farah (Kathy)—and two boys—Yousuf and Jacob. My cousins were more like siblings to me.

Uncle Khadouri changed his car every year to the latest model of Chevrolet. Everyone in the city knew Khadouri Chinku's car because of its low license plate number (743). He was called Khadouri Chinku because his business was buying and selling *chinku* (scrap metal). He always sat in the back seat, on the right side of the car, leaning his head toward the window. Hussein, his chauffeur for many years, was treated as a member of the family.

Uncle Khadouri and family. Left to right: Jack, Kathy, Aunt Simha, Naomi, Uncle Kadouri, Lydia, and Joseph.

Aunt Simha was a tough lady who always knew everything that was going on but kept it under wraps. When she and my uncle went out one evening, we tipped Hussein to drive us to Abu Yonan (a hamburger joint). Aunt Simha did not approve because the meat there was not kosher, but she pretended not to know. She also found out that I had always wanted a white dishdasha, so she sewed one for me, which I loved and wore at home.

Friday nights were movie nights. I do not know how both our families fit in my uncle's Chevrolet, but we somehow did. Two loges were reserved for us every Friday evening at Al Khayam, the newest and best movie theater in Baghdad at the time. Aunt Simha would sit next to my mother and read the subtitles to her, and my uncle would do the same for Dad.

Aunt Simha with family and friends at the birth of
Jack in the hospital, 1955. I am in the middle of my
cousins. Naima is on the right.

We went on picnics together in one car. My cousin Kathy
and I used to lie down on the deck between the back seat and
the back windshield. It was fun. Who thought about safety and
seat belts in those days?

Every morning in the summer, my cousins and I swam in
the Dejla River. We would go early in the morning and get on
a rented rowboat that would take us to the middle of the river,
where we would swim.

One morning while my parents were still in London, my
cousin Kathy and I missed the excursion because we had to take
a test before entering middle school at Frank Iny to determine
our major: science or business. That was Monday, July 14,1958,
the day that changed life in Iraq forever.

Hussein, my uncle's chauffeur, drove us to the school early in the morning. As we approached a major roundabout, we saw that the roads were blocked by tanks and soldiers with machine guns.

"Where are you going?" one of the soldiers shouted as he stopped our car.

"Taking the children to school," Hussein answered as he rolled down his window.

"No school today, go back to your home," the soldier said.

Aunt Simha was surprised as she opened the door. "Why are you back?" she asked. "You are going to be late!" When Hussein recounted what happened, Aunt Simha was incredulous. She ran to the radio.

"The monarchy has been overthrown," the broadcaster on the radio announced enthusiastically. "This is now the Great Republic of Iraq." The radio station broadcast martial music all day, interrupted by the reading of telegrams from army divisions around the country pledging their allegiance to the new government.

We stayed home and watched the news on television. All members of the royal family were executed, and the regent was killed. His body was dragged on the streets, then hung on the Ministry of Defense building, with his genitals cut off and stuffed in his mouth. We were terrified. The king was only twenty-three, and the country was getting ready to celebrate his wedding to a Turkish princess. No one knew what to expect with the military taking over the government.

"Oh my God, they killed the king," Aunt Simha kept saying throughout the day.

One day later the prime minister, Nuri al-Said, was found

in a souk disguised as a woman. He was shot, and his body was dragged through the streets, mutilated, and burnt beyond recognition.

I was terrified. My parents were out of the country, and we had no way to contact them. Aunt Simha was very comforting, and my cousins were really supportive.

Slowly the country settled down. Brigadier Abd al-Karim Qasim was appointed by the military as the country's new prime minister. Qasim was a nationalist, and during his rule, from 1958 to 1963, the Jews experienced less persecution and more freedom and were allowed to travel abroad and attend public colleges. The community felt more comfortable and participated in the national celebrations. Many families emigrated, and young people left for Europe and the States to continue their higher education.

In London Mom's condition was not improving. One day she called Aunt Simha from the hospital and told her that she believed she had had a shock in her doctor's office a few months before. She asked Aunt Simha to *tedahena* (oil her), a ritual everyone believed would cure the person from a trauma they had experienced.

Aunt Simha, as per Mom's instructions, went to the doctor's office and poured a small cup of oil mixed with water on a step on the stairs leading to the office. She placed her fingers in the oil mixture and recited specific prayers mentioning the name Naima, *bint* (daughter of) Chahla. Usually, the person doing the ritual would touch the oil on the floor and lightly place it on the patient's hands and forehead, which was obviously not possible at that time. Aunt Simha called Mom on the same day to tell her she had done the ritual. Strangely enough, Mom's condition started to improve, and she started to move her lower limbs. That is the power of belief.

Mom came back to Baghdad walking with the help of a cane. I moved back home with my parents, and after a few months, Mom did not need the cane anymore. Our life went back to normal.

CHAPTER 8

London, 1961

"Come here, *ibni*," Naeem, Dad's business partner, called to me. I was playing with the other kids, zigzagging between the café's tables. Naeem and Dad were standing with several men around a small table watching a game of backgammon. Naeem handed Dad his small coffee cup to hold and reached out to feel a little lump above my throat with his fingers.

"Abu Saleh, feel this lump," Naeem said to Dad. "It's like a big pea." Dad felt the lump in my neck with his fingers and shook his head.

"We need to show it to a doctor," he said.

The doctor diagnosed the lump as a cyst. "Don't worry," the doctor told Mom. "During the formation of the thyroid gland in some babies, the duct between the base of the tongue and the thyroid gland sometimes does not disappear and a pocket of saliva forms; we call it a thyroglossal cyst." The doctor further explained, "It's a simple procedure to remove the cyst and the duct." My parents were relieved, and the surgery was scheduled.

On the day of the surgery, Mom took me to the hospital. We checked in at the reception and were told to go to the waiting room. I was nervous and scared, and Mom held my hand in hers trying to calm me.

"Yousuf," a nurse standing at the door to the waiting room called. Mom and I stood up. "I will take him from here," she told Mom. "You can wait here."

I followed the nurse, looking back at Mom, who smiled and nodded her head and reassured me with her eyes. I felt my heart pounding in my chest.

"Walk down the corridor," the nurse said, "and at the end you will see a double door, that's the operating room. The doctor is waiting for you there." She turned around and left. I walked toward the double door in a cloud. The corridor looked very long. I ran my fingers over the mass on my neck. I imagined the surgeon sliding a knife across my neck. I trembled like a sheep on its way to be slaughtered. Inside the operating room, everything was white, and the lights above the operating table were very bright. A doctor in a white robe and a mask on his face was waiting by the table. A nurse helped me take off my T-shirt and get on the table. The doctor didn't even look at me. He was joking with a second nurse who was standing by a monitor.

The doctor raised a syringe up in the air and squirted some liquid out before he finally turned to me. "Yousuf, I am going to give you an injection to relax you," he said as he stuck the needle in my arm. "Count from ten down to one."

"Ten, nine, eight, seven . . ." My vision became blurry. "Six . . . five . . . four . . ."

When I opened my eyes, Mom was sitting next to my bed, smiling.

"You are all done, the cyst is gone, and in a few days you will be back home."

One week later, the bandages were removed, revealing a four-inch scar adorning my neck.

The following winter I came down with a severe cold. A bubble formed at the middle of the scar on my neck. After a few days, the bubble popped open, and mucus flowed down my neck. The doctors consulted said that the thyroglossal duct had not been removed completely, and saliva filled the remaining portion, which then found a weak spot to burst open. They all agreed that I needed another surgery to fix the problem. The surgeon who did the first operation recommended a well-known surgeon in London who specialized in thyroid issues.

We could travel out of the country for medical treatment as long as a member of the family stayed home to ensure our return. I had stayed home with my uncle's family when Mom and Dad traveled to London a few years before; this time Dad stayed home.

Mom and I flew on an Iraqi Airways Viscount plane to London. Everyone on the plane was frightened and quiet for the first leg of the voyage. Colonel Fadhil Abbas al-Mahdawi, a notorious military judge known for sentencing politicians associated with the previous regime to death, and his entourage were on the plane. When they got off the plane in Budapest, a stop the plane made on the way to London, everyone on the plane felt relieved.

Albert I., the friend of the family who handled our correspondence with my siblings in Israel, met us at the London airport. It was drizzling, and the wet streets reflected the lights of the traffic signals. As we had no traffic signals in Baghdad at the time, I did not understand why Albert stopped the car every time the light turned red and waited for it to turn green, because for God's sake, there was no one on the streets!

The next morning, we saw the surgeon at his office on Harley Street, and I was admitted to the hospital. Unlike the nurses back home, the nurses in London were very nice to me; they helped dissipate my fears and calmed me down. They were fascinated by the fourteen-year-old boy from Iraq who spoke fluent English. "Do you have a camel?" one young nurse asked me. She was serious. *How come we knew so much more about Britain than the British knew about Iraq?* I wondered.

The surgeon wanted me to stay in London for three months so he could monitor my recovery. Mom and I did lots of sightseeing, shopping, and socializing with Iraqi friends who lived in London at that time. These were wonderful and carefree days for me, but not for Mom, who was very worried about Dad back home.

One morning Albert called and told Mom that Saleh was in London for the day on business. What a coincidence. Mom had not seen Saleh since he left the house with Dad eleven years before. She was very eager to see him. When Mom saw Saleh, she started crying and hugged him for a long time. I do not remember what they talked about. Our meeting was very short because Saleh had to catch a flight. I did not grasp at the time how important the few minutes we spent with Saleh were. I was too young and could not think of Saleh as a brother.

Finally, the surgeon said we could go home. I wanted to fly on the new Boeing 707, so I took Mom to Pan American Airways'

London.

office to change our tickets. We both stood to admire a big model of the Boeing 707 that sat prominently in the center of the office. Our flight to Baghdad with one stop in Frankfurt would take six hours. I was so excited and could not wait to get on that plane.

The flight to Frankfurt took one hour. Then came the bad news: The plane would not continue its flight because of engine problems. The next flight would be one week later. We stayed in Frankfurt for two days while the airline company scrambled to find us a flight back home with no stop in an Arab country, fearing for our safety as Jews. Finally, they put us on a Swiss Air flight to Baghdad through Geneva. Flying on a Caravelle plane was very exciting. *Lucky me,* I thought, *I have experienced them all—the Viscount, the Boeing 707, and the Caravelle.*

We arrived in Baghdad at midnight. I looked out of the plane window expecting to see a city full of lights, but Baghdad was a big, dark area lit by only a few lights flickering here and there.

No one met us at the airport because the city was under curfew. We took a taxi home.

Two years after returning from London, I got a severe cold, and my neck swelled up again. A hole in my surgery incision burst open, and mucus started running down my neck again. I had to wrap my neck with a handkerchief all the time to collect the mucus. The surgeon in London said, "Maybe the thyroid duct was not removed completely." *Again?* He talked to the surgeon who did the first surgery in Baghdad and instructed him how to drain the duct. Once a week for a few months, the local surgeon drained the fluid from the duct using a syringe, a very painful procedure.

I took the national baccalaureate exam in the midst of the draining process. I had to change the wrap around my neck two or three times during the test. By the end of 1963, the fluid stopped running and the hole in my neck healed. I lived with this problem for the next ten years until I had a third surgery in Los Angeles.

CHAPTER 9

Elementary and High School, 1952–1963

After the Big Aliyah in 1951–52, only two Jewish schools remained operational in Baghdad: Menahem Daniel elementary (kindergarten through sixth grade) and Frank Iny School (kindergarten through twelfth grade). Menahem Daniel elementary was in a nondescript building with a small playground in downtown Baghdad. The Frank Iny School campus was located in Alwiyah, a suburb of Baghdad, and consisted of an L-shaped two-story building, accessory buildings, and a soccer field.

I attended both schools for my elementary and high school education. For the next twenty years, all the community children (except for the few who went to other private schools) went to one or both of these schools since public schools did not accept Jewish kids.

In addition to the curriculum set by the government, the two schools taught the English and French languages from kindergarten through twelfth grade (sixth grade at Menahem

Daniel) and the history of Europe. In middle and high school, all science classes were taught in French in the tenth grade, in English in the eleventh grade, and in Arabic in the twelfth grade. In addition to the baccalaureate national test to graduate high school in Iraq, Frank Iny students had to take and pass the same tests that students took in high schools in Britain and France.

The two schools were well known locally and abroad for their high academic level, and many prominent people and government officials enrolled their children there. In hindsight, the community schools were preparing us to finish our higher education and to live in Europe or the United States.

The Principals

Mrs. Qanawaty, the principal of Menahem Daniel, was short and heavy. She was friendly and caring but very strict. She walked around the school and into classrooms regularly. I can still see her sitting behind a large desk in her office addressing Mom and me as we sat across from her.

Mr. Ovadia, the principal of Frank Iny school, was five-foot-six and skinny. He was very strict and was feared by the students. He walked around the school every hour with his hands in his pockets to check on the classrooms, and God help any student he saw out of the classroom.

Nothing escaped Mr. Ovadia. A few of us skipped school one day and went to see a movie. During the intermission we were shocked to see Mr. Ovadia walk across the theater with his hands in his pockets, looking at us, making sure we saw him. We expected the worst, but he did nothing; he made his point.

The only time I remember Mr. Ovadia smiling at me was after I graduated college when I went to see him in his office to ask him for recommendations for higher studies. Twenty years later, the students of Frank Iny traveled from all over to Montreal for a reunion to honor Mr. Ovadia. We all realized that he was doing his job educating us and that he made us who we are today.

My First Day of School

"Today you are a big boy," Mom told me on my first day of school. "You will make new friends, and you will play and learn. You are so lucky. I am so proud of you." It was the fall of 1952.

I stood next to Mom, who sat on a bench in the playground next to another woman with a young girl on her lap. I watched

Me at six years old.

the boys and girls running around and playing on the playground. When a bell rang, all the children ran into the two buildings. Mom and her new lady friend got up, and we walked to a large room that faced the playground. The room was full of children my age. Mom sat next to me and the other kids at a low table while a teacher was talking. I was fascinated. The walls were covered with pictures of flowers, butterflies, and kids playing. On one wall there were lots of letters and symbols.

"I will be back in an hour," Mom said to me as she got up. I nodded, and she left the room; I was too busy absorbing my surroundings.

The French teacher, Sit (Ms.) Alice, a short, heavyset woman with short hair and thick glasses, approached me. She had cards with big letters in her hand. She came so close to me that I could feel her breath.

"Aah . . . beh . . . ceh . . . deh . . ." she recited in a loud voice. That day, she had me repeat the whole French alphabet after her. When Mom came to pick me up, I did not want to leave.

Every morning after that, a rickety school bus full of children picked me up at home. On the bus we played games and chatted. Mom waited with me for the school bus by the gate to our yard, with a tall glass of milk and tea. "Drink it," she would say. "It will make you strong, so you will not need the vitamin B injection." The doctor gave me that injection in my buttock twice a month, because he thought I was too skinny for my age. The injection was so painful that it made me limp for days. That was enough to scare me into drinking the milk.

The Rose

In second grade, Sit Mosli, the principal's assistant, whispered some words in the teacher's ear and left the class as abruptly as she walked in.

"Yousuf, Sit Mosli wants to see you after classes today." Everyone in the classroom looked at me. *Why does Sit Mosli want to see me? Did I do anything wrong?* A boy in the back said something and the few that heard him laughed.

After class I stood in the school lobby while the other kids ran out of the building. *I will miss the bus,* I thought. The custodian closed the door behind him and left the building. It seemed like I was the only one in the school. You could hear a pin drop.

Sit Mosli came down the curved stairs from the second floor and motioned for me to come closer. She looked very tall. She wore a brown woolen dress, and her left arm was behind her back.

"What is this?" she asked as her left hand came out of hiding with a fresh red rose. I looked at the flower. "What is this?" she asked again.

"A red rose," I answered.

"Is it beautiful?"

I hesitated and nodded my head.

"Does it smell good?"

I nodded again.

"What if we pull out the rose's petals just for fun?" She waited, but no answer came. I was frozen.

"Of course, we don't do that. We should be gentle with a rose," Sit Mosli said as she caressed the rose. "We should take care of it." She paused for an eternity. Then she said, "You pushed

Stella in the playground today, and she fell and hurt her knee."
Oh, that's why I am here.

"A girl is just like a rose, tender and beautiful. Boys must be gentle with girls and take care of them." She looked at me and waited to see if I absorbed her lesson. I nodded my head.

"You must always be gentle with girls. Never push or hit a girl." She paused and then said, "I called your mother to pick you up."

I walked away thinking, *I like roses, but I do not like girls!*

Little did I know that in a few years I would like girls more than roses!

Punishment

Our Hebrew teacher in fifth grade, Ustadh (Professor) Yakub Seraj, was an elderly man who wore thick prescription glasses and wobbled when he walked due to his weight. Learning the Hebrew language was forbidden, so our Hebrew studies were limited to learning to read the prayers without even understanding what they meant.

One day Ustadh Seraj was walking between the rows of desks, slowly tapping his left hand with a wooden ruler he was holding in his right hand. He stopped in front of my desk and pointed his ruler at me.

"Yousuf, recite the Shema," he ordered, looking me in the eyes.

I stood up and started, *"Shema Israel, Adhonai eluhenu, adhonai ehad."* I sat down, relieved.

"Continue!" he said in a loud voice.

I felt a shiver go through my body as I stood up again. "*Baroukh . . . Kebod . . .*" I drew a blank, I was so nervous.

"Go on." He came closer. "Go on. . . ."

I froze. His face turned red, and I could see he was getting angry.

"Get up, stand on the bench, come on!" he said.

With tears running down my cheeks, I climbed onto my bench. He started hitting me on my hamstrings with the edge of the ruler. He counted ten strikes.

"Sit down, and next time do your homework," he barked as he walked away. The class was quiet. I went home limping. When I told Mom what happened, she was enraged. In the morning, she took me to the school and met with the principal, Mrs. Qanawaty, and Ustadh Seraj and made it clear that hitting children was not acceptable. Ustadh Seraj never hit students after that.

Teachers

Hitting or slapping students was acceptable. Mr. Sopher, our trigonometry teacher in eleventh grade, was different. When Mr. Sopher turned to write on the chalkboard, students walked around the class and threw chalk at the chalkboard. Mr. Sopher, a short and stocky man, turned around, straightened his prescription eyeglasses on his nose, ran to the first student who he made eye contact with, took all books and notes on top of that desk, and threw them out of the second-floor window. It was hilarious.

Getting in Trouble

Life during school was exciting. In the classroom, students did what all students do—passed written messages and misbehaved when the teacher was not looking. Everyone carved their name, hearts, or flowers into their desktops.

I was always one of the top students in class, but I did get in trouble a few times during my high school years. In eighth grade, I was suspended from school for three days. Our French teacher, Madame Therese, caught me and Albert (who later became my brother-in-law) laughing. She sent us down to the principal's office. Mr. Ovadia and his top assistants, Usthadh Is'hak and Sit Simha, decided to suspend us for three days and sent us home.

Albert and I walked to his house. Albert's mother was very understanding, she was not upset. We sat with her on the large swing in their front yard and chatted. I was very nervous. *What do I tell my parents?* I was thinking.

"It's not the end of the world," Albert's mom said. "Just go home, your mom is cool." She was right. When I told my mom that I was suspended from school because of a comment I whispered into Albert's ear, she just laughed. She did not even tell Dad.

First Sex Lesson

My first sex lesson did not come in the classroom. Sex was a taboo subject that was not discussed in the presence of children. My parents never talked about sex with me. Like the others, I learned about sex (the right and the wrong) from older kids or from books.

One afternoon my friend Azouri and I were playing in the front yard of his home, which was surrounded by a high wall like all houses in Baghdad. I was seven, Azouri was eight. We went to the gate to watch the neighborhood kids playing on the street.

"See that girl and boy?" Azouri pointed to the balcony on the second floor of the house across the street. A boy and a girl were leaning against the balcony railing, laughing.

"*Houi yneeka* [He fucks her]," Azouri said, still looking at them.

"What does that mean?" I asked.

"He puts his penis in her butt."

Why would he do that? I thought. *That must be painful.*

Friends for Life

My lifelong special friendship with Edward Daoud and Edward Ezer was forged during these years and throughout high school. Sweet memories come alive when I remember us playing croquet and climbing the *nabugh* (cherrylike fruit) tree in the garden of Edward Ezer's house.

But there were some bad memories too. In fifth grade, Edward Ezer sat next to me in class. One day he stood up to recite a poem. In the meantime, I stood my pencil up on the bench, and when Edward sat down . . . ugh . . . he landed on the pencil. He jumped up screaming. Only then did I realize what I had done. The teacher punished me by making me stand in the corner of the classroom facing the wall.

Edward's mom called my mom to tell her what had happened. She had to take Edward to the doctor to have the pencil lead removed from his thigh. Mom grounded me for days with no phone and no visits to friends. I felt so guilty, and I apologized to Edward several times.

In eleventh grade, Edward Daoud and I were spotted by the teacher exchanging paper messages and were kicked out of the classroom. Not knowing what to do, we stood outside the classroom door and were caught by the principal, Mr. Ovadia, making his rounds.

"What are you doing outside the classroom?" Mr. Ovadia asked. Both Edward and I looked at the floor and said nothing.

"Yousuf, you are a good student. I am disappointed," Mr. Ovadia said as he pulled at my left ear. Out of the corner of his eye, he saw Edward laughing. He left me and turned to Edward, grabbed his right ear, and pulled it upward. Edward stood on his toes.

"You find this funny?" Mr. Ovadia asked. "Get back in class now and don't let me see you here during class again."

After that I learned my lesson—when kicked out of the classroom, I would go to the restrooms downstairs and hide for the duration of the class.

Social Life

Our lives as teenagers revolved around the *Mal'ab* (playground), the youth club run by the Jewish community. The large grounds had a track field and courts for basketball, volleyball, and tennis, as well as Ping-Pong tables. It was complete with a cafeteria and locker rooms. Coaches and trainers were available to everyone, and competitions in all sports were held every year. This was the outlet for Jewish kids since they had no place to go to after school and in the summer.

Parties were the other outlet. Kids invited their peers to a dance party at their homes, where the light would be dimmed and they would dance with their boyfriends and girlfriends to the latest British and American hits.

At sixteen I had a girlfriend for the first time. We talked a lot on the phone, went to the movies with other boys and girls, and spent time together at parties or at home with family members present. Such relationships were platonic—at most a stolen kiss in a secluded corner of the school.

Extracurriculars

Over the years, with the encouragement of the chemistry teacher, I built up my own chemistry lab at home. I used to run my own chemistry tests and write reports. Even though I was eager to pursue science, Dad wanted me to learn bookkeeping. He arranged for an accountant to teach me *blanjo* (double-entry bookkeeping) during the summer vacation. I biked to the tutor's home early in the morning twice a week. I did not retain much of what he taught me. Accounting never interested me.

A few months before I turned thirteen, Dad arranged for an older religious man to teach me the Jewish prayers and the Holy Days so I could have my Bar Mitzvah. I met the tutor at the Meir Tweg Synagogue in Bataween every day after the daily morning services and studied with him for over a month. On my birthday, he put the *tefillin* on me, and I read the *bracha* (blessing). The *tefillin*, a pair of small black boxes containing

Hebrew parchment scrolls attached to two leather straps, is worn by observant Jewish men every weekday.

"Mazel tov," the old man said. "You are a Bar Mitzvah now, and from now on you are responsible for all your actions." I went back home and told my parents that I had my Bar Mitzvah, but that I was not ready to be responsible for my actions. My parents laughed heartily.

CHAPTER 10

A Violent Year, 1963

In 1963, Iraq was shaken by two violent coups. The Ramadan Coup was led by the Ba'athists on February 8, 1963. Fighting went on for two days, and more than five thousand people were killed. The Ba'ath, a socialist party that called for the unification of the Arab world, seized power. Abd al-Karim Qasim, the popular nationalist leader, was killed, and his deputy, Abdul Salam Arif, was appointed as the new president. Arif and Qasim had led the earlier 1958 revolution that transformed Iraq from a parliamentary monarchy to an autocratic republic.

Once in power, the Ba'athists terrorized the population and went on a rampage to imprison and kill anyone suspected of being a Communist or simply an activist. Hundreds of thousands were massacred all over Iraq. Teenagers armed with machine guns, part of the newly formed People's Army, roamed the streets of Baghdad and other Iraqi cities, beating or shooting people at random. Internally the Ba'ath party was divided; some wanted to join Syria, while others wanted to continue the policies of Qasim: Iraq first.

The Ba'athists required Jews to carry yellow ID cards. The word *Moussawi* (follower of Moses) was written in big red letters on the front of the card, which had the photo, date of birth, and address of the person. The People's Army were stationed at every main street corner and stopped people they suspected. When they saw the yellow card, they usually became abusive, insulted the person, and sometimes spit on him or her, or even beat the person up.

In June of that year, I took the national baccalaureate test to graduate from high school. The testing location assigned to our Jewish school was in a Ba'athist suburb of Baghdad, not a good place for Jewish kids to be. For the six days of the test, we had to interact and take the test with Ba'athist teenagers who carried machine guns. Most mornings they would come to us before the test with the actual test problems, asking us for the solutions. In the classroom, they would have the test supervisor leave the room so they could walk around and copy our answers. We were very scared, but the armed teenagers were friendly because they needed us.

On November 12, 1963, Abdul Salam Arif, with the help of the military and his brother Abul Rahman Arif, ousted the Ba'ath leaders and established a pro-Nasser (Egypt's president at the time) regime. It took the military six violent days to suppress the Ba'ath National Guards who were in control of the streets in most Iraqi cities.

Before the Ba'athists put a stop to Jews leaving Iraq, many of my friends who graduated high school with me left for Europe or the States to continue their higher education. I had long discussions with my parents about us leaving the country.

"You can go, *ibni*, but I will stay and die here," Dad said. "Wherever we go, I will be dependent and a burden on others."

I tried, in vain, to assure him that I would always be with him and Mom, and that they would adjust to their new life. In my heart I understood Dad's thinking and would have done the same had I been in his shoes. After thinking long and hard, I decided to stay with my parents, knowing that if I left, I may never see them again. So I applied to Baghdad University.

Early one morning in August 1963, I went to a government office to get the *adam al mahkoomiah* certificate (no criminal record), required for admission to the university. The office was on the second floor, overlooking the courtyard on the first floor where people waited. I filled out my application for the certificate and handed it, along with the fee of one dinar, to a soldier who stood at the bottom of the stairs. The courtyard was packed; well-dressed students and shabbily dressed felons waited together. Some of the men lined the stairs to the second floor, leaning on the railing. There was no space to move.

Every thirty minutes or so, an officer in a military uniform came out to the balcony with a batch of papers in hand and shouted the applicants' names out loud. People whose names were called ran up the stairs to get their papers.

Around noon, the officer called my name: "Yousuf *Haskel*," he said, emphasizing the "Haskel," which is a common Jewish name. People around me started looking around to see who the Jew was. I was afraid to answer, so the officer shouted louder, "Yousuf *Haskel*! Where is that Jew?"

I joined the waiting crowd looking for *that Jew*. After a few moments, which seemed like hours, the officer moved on to call other names. I waited for an hour, climbed up the stairs, and knocked on the officer's door. "Excuse me, sir," I said, "I am Yousuf Haskel Dabby."

"You are the Jew," he said, looking at me from behind his desk. "I called your name several times."

"I am sorry, sir, I was in the restroom and did not hear you." My heart was beating fast. He picked up my papers, which were still on his desk, and gave them to me. I thanked him and ran down the stairs and out of the building.

Civil engineering was never my choice of a career. My first lesson in life: We dream and we plan, but life does what it wants. My dream since elementary school had been to study chemistry, however both the department of chemical engineering and the school of medicine (my second choice) at Baghdad University denied my application. I was told that Jews were not allowed to study these two fields, because they can help the enemy of the state, Israel.

CHAPTER 11

University, 1963–1967

In mid-September, after my application to Baghdad University was denied, I applied for admission to the College of Civil Engineering at Al-Hikma University. Al-Hikma, a private university built and run by American Jesuit fathers and affiliated with Boston College, accepted Jews and Kurds. It offered three majors: civil engineering, business management, and English literature.

On the morning of my interview, Mom was very nervous.

"I want you to keep this pellet in your mouth during the interview," Mom said, handing me a pebble-size round, metallic pellet.

"You must be kidding," I said. "How do you expect me to talk with this in my mouth?"

"Leave it in your cheek and forget about it. It is for good luck." She was very serious, and I figured I could use any help or good luck I could get.

My interview with the dean, Father Ryan, SJ, went well. With the pellet in my mouth, I spoke slowly and cautiously—maybe that was the purpose. I was admitted and started my freshman year one month after classes went in session.

To commute to college, Dad bought me my first car. It was a beige 1964 Morris Oxford. Within the week, I had my first car accident. The car ahead of mine accelerated, then stopped, and I just plowed into it. My parents did not make a big fuss, which made me feel even more guilty.

My four years in college were wonderful. I was one of those annoying students in class, always raising my hand and arguing with the teacher, especially in ethics and philosophy classes. I was involved in the yearbook committee, the photography club, the debating society, and theater. I founded the campus weekly newsletter entitled *HUT*, for *Handassah, Adaab, Tijarah* (engineering, literature, business). I was the editor of the newsletter and wrote a philosophical weekly essay dealing with life on campus. I called it *Da'ani antaleq* (Let me open up).

At university, 1964.

On stage at university.

College opened my eyes to life in the real world. Before college, my environment was limited. I had little contact with non-Jews because I was not allowed to go to public schools or to work in governmental offices or big businesses. My circle of friends consisted of the kids I went to school with and their siblings. At college, the student body was diverse, with people from different social, religious, and ethnic backgrounds. My best friends were a Sunni Muslim, Quraish; a Palestinian, Saleh; and an Armenian, Hilal. We studied together and traveled within the country together. The three of them spent more time in our house than in theirs, and Mom treated them as members of the family.

The Jesuit fathers were aware of the Jews' predicament and were very helpful. They encouraged me to apply to UCLA graduate school and got me admitted with a full scholarship. Unfortunately, I never got to use that opportunity because I could not leave Iraq for several years after graduating from Al-Hikma.

Father Jolson, SJ, helped us communicate with my brother, Saleh, in Los Angeles. Whenever he traveled to the States, he carried with him gifts and letters for Saleh. I regret that I could not reunite with any of the Jesuit fathers after graduating. I did visit Boston College and looked for anyone who had served in Baghdad, but at the time they had all been reposted to other places around the world. I am so sorry I could not thank them for all they did.

My family, 1965.

CHAPTER 12

The Six-Day War, June 5, 1967

The sunlight warmed up my face. I opened my eyes; the sunrays ran across the ceiling of my bedroom, casting a distorted shadow of the hanging light fixture. I checked my watch and jumped out of bed. I knew my friend Jack would be there to pick me up any minute. I changed my clothes and ran down the stairs.

"Good morning," Mom said as she looked at me with wonderment. "Breakfast?" She pointed at the breads, cheeses, and fruits spread out on the dining table.

"No time."

"What's the rush? Where are you going?"

"To the university," I mumbled, chewing on a piece of bread I grabbed from the table.

"I thought you were done with university."

"Yes, Mama, I am done with university, but today I am going to get my graduation gown, cap, and tassels."

"The graduation ceremony is on Saturday, right?"

"Yes, and you and Baba better be there."

"We wouldn't miss it for the world."

The sound of a car horn came from the street, two short blasts.

"Jack is here," I said, rushing out the door. "See you later."

Jack and I had been classmates for the past ten years in high school and university. We carpooled every day to the university, a thirty-minute drive, and today it was his turn to drive. Jack wore a crew cut hairstyle and was taller and heavier than me. He walked in a relaxed and leisurely way with a smile that never left his face.

I closed the garden gate behind me and got into Jack's car, a yellow 1964 Vauxhall Victor FB. Jack was dressed in a white short-sleeve button-up shirt. I wore a light-blue long-sleeved shirt that day. I never liked short-sleeve shirts.

"Are you ready for graduation?" Jack asked.

"I am ready, let's go." Jack shifted gears, and we were on our way. "Let's go to the cafeteria first," I suggested.

Jack parked the car by the College of Civil Engineering building, and we walked across the beautiful garden to the cafeteria. Walking toward us were our good friends Quraish and Saleh, who is a Palestinian.

"Hi, guys, where are you going?" I asked them as they got closer.

"Today we will throw you in the sea," Saleh said.

"All the Jews will soon be in the dustbin of the world!" Quraish added in an angry tone as both of them passed us without stopping.

"What is going on?" Jack asked. "Why didn't they even stop to greet us?"

We entered the cafeteria and joined a few classmates sitting around a table.

"Haven't you heard?" a classmate asked with exuberance.

"The war of liberation started," another classmate said.

"We attacked Israel, and *inshallah* [God willing] the Jews will be thrown in the sea where they belong," someone added from across the table.

It was very awkward. Everyone knew Jack and I were Jewish.

"Maybe we should go home," I whispered to Jack. We stood up and left.

On the way home, we were both quiet. Jack turned on the radio. Martial music came into the car. The music was interrupted by a very enthusiastic broadcaster.

"This is a big day, a day of victory and pride. Our planes are bombing Tel Aviv, and our tanks and soldiers are marching to take back our land, the land of Palestine. We will kill the Jews and destroy their cities." I turned the radio off.

"This is scary," I said. "We better get home quickly."

"What is it with Quraish and Saleh?" Jack asked. "I thought we were good friends."

The road back to the city was unusually deserted. Jack dropped me off at our street and drove off as I ran into the house.

"Mama, Mama where are you?" My mother was not on the first floor and not in the garden. I ran upstairs and saw the door to the roof open. I walked out onto the roof and immediately felt the scorch of the sun. It was around noon, and the temperature may have been over one hundred degrees.

Mom was in the water closet tearing papers and photos and throwing them in a large metal tub, where she had a small fire going. She wore a dark-blue apron on top of her gray dress, and her hair was disheveled, beads of sweat collecting on her forehead and her eyeglasses steamy.

"Mama, what are you doing?"

"Come, help me, don't just stand there," she answered without looking up. "The neighbor told me that the Arab armies are attacking Israel and they are already in Tel Aviv, haven't you heard?"

"I heard, but what are *you* doing?" I grabbed her arm.

"If *they* find these, we will be in big trouble." She pulled her arm away to empty the bowl full of burnt photos in the toilet bowl. "*They*" is how everyone referred to security police.

"We can't leave any trace of family in Israel or America in the house."

"But . . . but Mama," I said in disbelief, "these photos . . . these letters . . . they are all we have. . . ."

The black-and-white photos were our only remembrance of my siblings who left the country sixteen years before. But my mom was right—we had to get rid of them. So I stood next to her in the small water closet, taking photos from a paper bag and handing them to her after looking at each one, trying to have them imprinted in my mind. I was angry and felt pain in my heart.

"When I'm done here, I want you to hide my jewelry and some cash," Mom said.

After cleaning the area, I came down the stairs. Mom walked out of her bedroom with two small plastic bags in her hand.

"Let's go to the storage room," she said without stopping. The storage room was attached to the house and had its entry door off the patio. It was full of items that should have been trashed, but Mom never threw anything out.

"Here," Mom said, pointing at the floor in the corner of the room.

"Mama, this is a tiled floor, you want me to break the tile?"

"No, remove it carefully, dig a hole in the ground to hide these bags, and put the tile back on top." Mom knew exactly what she wanted.

"With what tools?" I asked. Mom gave me a look and left the room. With a screwdriver and a small hammer, all the tools I had, I removed the tile and dug a hole in the ground. I placed the two bags with Mom's jewelry and around two thousand dinars in the hole, then put enough dirt on top so the tile could sit flat. I used cement to grout around the tile.

Dad came home earlier than usual that day. He locked the gate and the main entry door as he came into the house.

"God help us, if what the radio is saying is true," he said. He sat in his usual chair by the radio. "We won't know the truth until Radio Israel comes through," he said while looking up with his arms up in the air, his way of communicating with God. Radio Israel broadcast in Arabic on medium frequency wave and could only be heard in Baghdad in the evenings.

Finally, the evening came, and with it came the reception of Radio Israel. "Early in the morning," the reporter said, "Israel launched preemptive air strikes and destroyed the air forces of Egypt, Jordan, and Syria." The broadcaster spoke slowly and calmly in Arabic. "Israeli cities were not touched," he said, "and the Israeli defense forces have already moved into Jordan's West Bank, Syria's Golan Heights, and Egypt's Sinai Peninsula." This was a different story from what we heard during the day. We felt a flood of relief.

"Israel is safe, thank you, God," Dad said, looking at the ceiling again and taking a deep breath. "Now we need You to watch over us."

"They don't need any excuse to attack us now." Mom mentioned *they* again.

"Let's stay home the next few days," Dad said, "until things clear."

We sat by the radio that evening and listened to the BBC and Voice of America. Both stations confirmed what Radio Israel said. We did not sleep that night or on the five nights that followed. No one left the house for the next five days.

The war (later called the Six-Day War) ended on Saturday, June 10, 1967. Israel took the Sinai Desert, crossed the Suez Canal into Egypt, took the West Bank and the Golan Heights, and celebrated the return of Jerusalem, while the Arab countries did not know how to explain their incredible defeat to their people.

CHAPTER 13

Imprisoned, July 5, 1967

It was one month to the day after the start of the war between Israel and five Arab countries: Iraq, Syria, Lebanon, Jordan, and Egypt. The Arab world was still in shock at their devastating loss. Iraqi Radio continued to play martial music interspersed with military announcements. The mood on the streets of Baghdad was somber. The small Jewish community—around two thousand at the time—was fearful and anxious. From past experience, every Israeli action triggered revenge against the Jews, so we feared the worst. We were waiting for the other shoe to drop.

"I am going to the café today," my father announced when he came back from work. "I have not been there for more than a month." Since the war started, we had not left home, except for my father, who went to his shop for a few hours every day. We wanted to be out of sight and hoped to stay out of trouble.

Mom was in her bedroom resting, and I lay on my bed trying to read, my mind swirling. Thirty days before, I had graduated from college with a bachelor of science in civil engineering. The graduation ceremony was canceled because of the war. *Will things go back to normal?* I wondered. *Will I find a job?* I doubted it. In reality, we were being held in a prison, and now the prison would get even smaller. We had no future in our own country.

Ding-dong. The doorbell interrupted my thoughts.

"Who can that be?" Mom asked as she got up to look. "*They* are here," she said in a low, quavering voice. *They* again?

The doorbell rang again. Cold sweat ran down my back. I ran to join Mom at her bedroom window, which faced the street. Two men in plain clothes were trying to open the gate. Behind them I could see three soldiers and a military truck.

Mom opened the front door and walked down the steps to the gate. I stood by the door.

"Open the gate!" one of the men shouted. "Is Yousuf here?"

"What do you want from him?" Mom asked with a shaking voice.

"We have orders to search the house."

"Search the house?" Mom asked. "Orders . . . ?"

"Open the gate!" the man shouted angrily while shaking the gate.

Mom opened the gate, and the five men ran up the three steps.

"Are you Yousuf?" the first man asked as he passed me.

"Yes."

"You and your mother stay here. Anyone else in the house?"

"No," Mom said.

Four of the men went into the house, leaving a soldier to watch the two of us. I could see the living room from where I was standing by the front door. One of the men took everything out of the credenza and threw it on the floor—phone books, photo albums, candy boxes, and other items that Mom had neatly stored in there. Mom started bawling, and she sat down on the steps. I felt violated and helpless.

The men went in every room, ransacking the house, and we could not do a thing.

After what seemed like an eternity, they walked out, each of them carrying a bunch of papers, books, and photos.

"You"—the man pointed at me—"come with us."

"Why?" Mom pleaded.

"*Ukhti* [My sister], don't worry," one of the men in plain clothes said in a soft voice. "We need to ask him a few questions. We will bring him back in a few hours."

"I am coming with him," Mom said.

"*La, ukhti* [No, my sister], you stay here. Don't worry, we will take good care of your son."

I climbed in the back of the military truck with the three soldiers. I looked back and saw Mom standing by the gate with a handkerchief in her hand. She looked lost and helpless. I wondered if I would ever see her again.

The truck took us to the Al-Rasheed Air Base, about five miles south of Baghdad. We were waved in at the gate of the base, and the truck stopped at a one-story office building, where the two men in plain clothes got off. The truck's next stop was at one of the many simple, one-story buildings scattered all over the base. The soldiers led me in and locked the metal door behind me.

Sitting on the concrete floor were Jack S., Fouad Y., Adil M., and Albert M., all Jewish students with me in college.

"Oh my God, how long have you guys been here?" I asked.

"Couple of hours," Jack answered.

"Did they tell you why they brought us here?" Fouad asked.

"No."

The room was bare except for a urinal and water closets in one corner. A cool breeze came through two window openings in one of the walls. Two young soldiers looked in through one of the openings with curiosity.

"Are you the Israeli pilots that bombed H3?" one of the soldiers asked. H3 was an Iraqi air base near the Iraqi-Syrian border. Rumor had it that an Israeli fighter plane had been shot down in that area and two Israeli pilots were captured.

"No, we are Iraqis like you," I answered. They shrugged and walked away.

Everyone in the room had been taken from their homes just like me, their houses were ransacked, and their families were told they would only be gone for a few hours.

It was getting dark quickly, and the only light in the room came from a light pole outside. Fouad and Albert lay down on the concrete floor. Jack and Adil sat down with their legs crossed. I paced the room back and forth. As it got darker, the cockroaches appeared. Everyone got up in horror.

"How are we going to sleep?" Fouad asked. That night and the nights that followed we shared the dusty concrete floor with the cockroaches and other insects. We got accustomed to them very quickly.

As I lay awake on the floor that first night, I thought about my parents and how they were handling the situation. I thought about our ransacked home and wondered who helped Mom to put everything back where it belonged. I could only imagine my father's shock when he came home and heard what happened. I wondered what would happen to us.

Why did the two soldiers think we were the Israeli pilots? I thought. *There were other Jewish students in college. Why the five of us?* Jack and Fouad were fellow civil engineering graduates. Adil was a junior in the College of Civil Engineering. We did not know Albert personally, but we knew he was a sophomore in the College of Business. Both Jack and Fouad were athletic, big, and muscular from weight training. I was thin and anything but athletic. Adil was dark-skinned and on the heavy side. Albert was heavyset and short.

The five of us were active on campus. Albert was known as Albert Abu al Thalij (owner of the ice) for his constant bragging that his family supplied all the ice in Baghdad. Adil was a good guitar player and sang Western hits at campus events. Jack headed the debating society and was a member of the drama club and on the board of the campus newsletter. Fouad was active in sports, and thanks to his loud motorcycle, he was known to everyone on campus as Fouad Abu al Mator (owner of the motorcycle).

The sudden sound of the door bursting open woke me up. I must have dozed off. It was still dark. Three men were standing at our heads—a tall, dark-skinned man in a military suit with stars on his shoulders and two soldiers with black sticks in their hands.

One of the soldiers prodded Fouad with his stick. "Get up . . . NOW! Stand up!"

We all stood up. We must have looked really disheveled.

"How does it feel to sleep on the floor?" the captain with a scar on his right cheek asked. "You will never sleep on a bed again." He laughed loudly, and the two soldiers joined him.

"Did you think you could get away with it?" the captain blared. "Filthy Jews, the scum of the earth, spies for the Americans." His eyes scanned each of us. "We will hang you one by one, *ya khawat al gahba* [brothers of a prostitute]."

Boom! A loud noise interrupted the captain. Fouad fell to the ground and was clearly unconscious. He must have fainted. The captain signaled to the soldiers to check on him. As they approached him, Fouad opened his eyes and looked around. He did not seem to know what happened. The soldiers helped him up.

"Ha ha ha." The captain laughed again. "Look at the *mukhanath* [weakling]. He looks tough—big and full of muscles— but he is nothing more than a *kharoof* [sheep]." He pointed at Fouad. "Bring him to my office; let's start with him," he told the soldiers and walked out of the room.

The four of us left in the room looked at each other.

"Spies for the Americans? Is that what they accuse us of? What are we going to do?" asked Jack with his hand on his head.

"Don't worry, my mom knows everyone, she will get us out," Albert said nonchalantly.

"I hope they don't hurt our parents," Adil said with concern.

Around midmorning, a soldier came to the window carrying a brown paper bag.

"A woman brought you food last night," he said as he handed me the paper bag. I could tell it was from my mom. In the bag there were sandwiches, apples, oranges, and soft drinks. At that moment food was the last thing on anyone's mind, although we had not even had a drink of water for the last twenty hours.

We were very scared and anxious. *What if they don't bring Fouad back? What if they torture him or kill him?* Everyone in the room was quiet, but I am sure everyone was thinking the same.

Six hours later they brought Fouad back. He was exhausted. We sat around him as he lay down on the floor. I opened a soft drink can and gave it to him. We were quiet and waited for him to say something. He took a sip.

"They . . . wanted me to say . . . that I helped Father Nash [one of the Jesuit fathers at the college]. . . . That I gave him photos I took of the base. . . ." Fouad struggled as he went on to tell us that they did not let him rest for one minute. They were nice to him at first, then they were rude and violent. They slapped him twice but did not torture him. He told them that in his four years at college he never took a photo and never talked to Father Nash, not even once.

"The captain told me, 'Next time, if you do not confess, we will finish you,'" Fouad recounted. "They have Hilda S. here too." Hilda was a sophomore in the College of Business. We were shocked. It was not common to interrogate or imprison women.

"Are you sure?" asked Jack.

"That's what they told me. They said she will easily confess."

We were speechless. A pretty Jewish girl in their hands—a frightening thought. We all knew what these people could and would do.

One by one we were all interrogated. I was the third one to go after Fouad and Jack. The captain sat at his desk, and two men in plain clothes sat on one of the two brown couches in the room. I was seated on a chair facing all three men. Behind me stood two rough-looking soldiers.

"We know the American Jesuits are spies, and we know that

you helped them to spy on our country," the captain started. "If you help us, we will be lenient with you and your friends." The two men on the couch nodded their heads.

"I am not a spy. I do not know or help any spies—"

"You are a spy. We have information that you and your friends are working for the Americans. How much did they pay you?"

"I do not work for the Americans. No one paid me. I am not a spy," I insisted.

This went on, and soon both the accusations and the threats got more serious.

"You took photos of the base," one of the men on the couch said. "You gave them to Father Nash."

"I never took photos of the base. I only took photos of other students on the campus, and the photos were for the yearbook."

"You built a model of the Hindiya Barrage," the captain said. "You were working with the American spies on a plan to destroy the barrage. Confess and we will not hurt you." The Hindiya Barrage was a dam that was built across the Euphrates River in 1913 to control the flooding that happened every year in the area.

"No, I did not build a model of the barrage," I explained. "My graduation thesis was about hydraulic jumps and waves, not about barrages. I made a model of a spillway to learn about the behavior of water." I think that explanation only made the situation worse for me.

This went on for hours, with threats of solitary imprisonment and torture. Finally, they gave me a typewritten confession to sign. It stated that I helped the American Jesuits to spy on Iraq and was planning to destroy important national installations with them. I refused to sign it.

"We have not started with you yet," the captain said. "Once we kill one of you, the rest will all confess and write their own confessions."

I was taken back to our cell.

Jack's graduation thesis was also used to incriminate him. His thesis was about type-A airport runways. Jack was told that the drawings and designs he made were drawings of the runways on the H3 air base, which had just been bombed by Israel, and that he had prepared the drawings for the American and Zionist spies.

After the five of us were interrogated, we were taken to the captain's office. The captain was standing by his desk and asked us to sit on the two brown couches in front of his desk. He proceeded to tell us that he had interrogated Father Nash and a few of our friends and that there was no doubt in his mind that both we and the American Jesuits were spies. He said that the information we had handed over to the Americans was damaging to the country's security. The captain gave us an ultimatum.

"I have no more patience with you, *awlad al gahba* [sons of a prostitute]," he said angrily. "You have till the end of the day to sign your confessions. If you don't . . ." He stood up and leaned on his desk. "*Wallah al Adhim* [In the name of God almighty], if you don't, I will make sure you leave this place in boxes."

The following morning one of the soldiers guarding our room told us that plans were made to execute us that evening. That day we got to know each other intimately. There was no fear and no embarrassment. We talked about our families, our friends, and our memories, both the happy and the sad. We laughed together and commiserated together. It was a very long day, but no one came for us. We thought they were bluffing.

At dawn the next morning, four soldiers showed up and ordered us to follow them.

They had us climb onto the back of a military truck and drove us out of the base. It was dark; the stars filled the clear sky, and the moon was just a sliver. The truck took us to an open, unpaved area surrounded by tall trees. The smell of manure permeated the still air.

They made us get off the truck and stood us against a mud wall. I was standing between Jack and Fouad. They shined the truck lights on us, so we could only see their silhouettes standing between us and the truck. My heartbeat quickened. *So, this is the end*, I thought. In that moment, I saw my life go by—my parents, my teachers, myself as a child running after my dog. . . .

"Will you sign your confessions?" someone asked in a loud voice. No one answered.

"Get ready to shoot the bastards." The same voice directed the soldiers.

I braced myself and held my breath. I wondered, *Will I hear the sound of the gunshots before I die? Will I feel pain?*

After what felt like an eternity, the group of men watching us burst into laughter. We were in shock.

"Move it," one of the soldiers ordered us. I walked back to the truck in a haze. During the ride back I was numb.

Back in the room, Jack said, "This was worse than the real thing."

How can a human being be so cruel to a fellow human being? But are these people humans? I wondered. To this day, this traumatic experience continues to haunt me. Once in a while I wake up in the middle of the night to the sound of gunshots, sweating profusely, and the smell of manure in my nose.

After that night we were left alone. We lived with the uncertainty of our fate. Food came daily from our families. Fouad led us in exercise every morning. Somehow the time passed, and life became a routine.

On the evening of July 23, 1967, the eighteenth day of our detention, we were taken to the captain's office again. Hilda was already there, standing by the door. We walked into the office expecting the worst. To our surprise we saw three of our mothers sitting on the brown couches, the captain at his desk, and two soldiers standing by him. My mother smiled as she saw me. Her eyes said, "Everything is okay."

"Your families have appealed to us to set you free," the captain said. "And we decided to let you go." He looked down at his desk and started to write.

The silence was broken by my mother. "*Hadhrat al-Dhabet* [Honorable officer], we thank you for releasing our kids, but how do we know that a different security agency won't come to take them again tomorrow or the next day?"

"Good question," the captain replied, looking up and thinking for a moment. "I will send a letter to all security agencies to inform them that we have investigated these young men and this young lady, and we found them innocent. I will give you a copy of that letter."

We, the "innocent young men and young lady," looked at each other with amazement. The captain was so smooth and gentle. He dictated a letter to his assistant and, in no time, handed my mom a yellow carbon copy of a letter cc'd to a dozen different security agencies. We were all escorted to the gate of the base, where a couple of the fathers were waiting to drive us home.

That evening I went to my cousin Farah's home to attend the *brit* (circumcision) of Farah and Sabah's first child, Elias. It was a double celebration for my family.

In the following weeks and months, what happened to us happened to many other members of our community. It turns out that Captain Ahmad al-Azawi Abu al-Jibin found a way to enrich himself. Every other week he arrested five or six Jews, held them in the military base, and released them when their families paid him his established fee. We learned that an esteemed member of the community, Mr. Samra, was the captain's messenger. Mr. Samra collected the ransom demanded by the captain, 250 dinars per person, from the families of the imprisoned and facilitated the release of their loved ones. There were those who believed that he pocketed some of the money, but most of us did not buy that and believed that Mr. Samra was a good man who used his connections to help the community.

One afternoon a few weeks later, I stopped at a gas station to fill up my car. I saw Quraish pumping gas in his car on the other side of the station. Quraish was the good friend who confronted me and Jack on campus on the day the war started. Our eyes met for a second, but he pretended not to see me. I was hurt and felt betrayed. Later, I heard that he might have been one of those who testified against us. I am certain that whatever he did was done for fear of his life, and that on the day we saw each other, he was afraid or maybe just embarrassed to talk to me.

CHAPTER 14

Pursuing My Career

I started looking for a job, but my search was frustrating and in vain. People were afraid to hire Jews. I freelanced here and there; I helped a Jewish engineer and followed another one supervising the construction of a building.

At a wedding party Dad asked the host, a contractor, if he could help me find a job. The host introduced me to his Christian partner. Jewish businesspeople partnered with non-Jews who would front their ventures, get the licenses, and secure the contracts.

"In fact, I just started a big road construction project in Al-Mansour [a suburb of Baghdad], and I could use an engineer," the partner said. "But I will have to pay him under the table, you know."

Paying under the table meant paying less than the going rate for an engineer, but I was happy. The job was to supervise the grading, compaction, and asphalt paving of roads in a new neighborhood. Every morning a pickup truck transported me and the workers to the jobsite. We all sat in the back, which was covered with canvas that did not do much to protect us from the cold. On the way to work, I discussed the day's scope of work with the superintendent. On the way back home, I wrote out the scope of work for the following day in the superintendent's notebook.

At the jobsite I surveyed the area, marked the road's boundaries and grades, supervised the grading work, and verified that the completed sections of the road complied with the plans. The city engineer and I shared an office near the jobsite. We met daily to discuss the job and its progress. He did not know that I was Jewish.

The heavy equipment—graders, bulldozers, sheepsfoot rollers, and trucks were guarded at night by a few Bedouin men who stayed in tents at the jobsite. The Bedouin guards were well-built, tall, strong, and armed. I visited with them every day, bringing gifts and checking on their needs, and I paid them weekly. We chatted, drank tea, and smoked together.

One morning, a month into the job, I asked the driver of the grader to re-excavate and regrade a portion of a road for the second time. He turned red with anger and jumped down from his high grader cabin. He had in his hand a stick with tar sculpted as a ball at its end. He headed toward me with the weapon. I started running, and he ran behind me, screaming, "*Yahoodi, ibn al gahba* [Jew, son of a prostitute], I will beat the crap out of you!"

How did he find out I was Jewish? Who else know? Where can I seek help now? My mind was running faster than my legs. *Maybe the Bedouins will help.* I ran into the Bedouins' tent. One of the Bedouin guards stood up and stopped the enraged man from coming into the tent. "Don't you dare touch the *muhandes* [engineer]," the Bedouin told the grader driver in a loud voice. "Go back to work."

I was trembling. The Bedouins offered me tea and a cigarette. I called the contractor and asked him to send a car to pick me up. That was the end of that job.

Without a job I had a lot of time to kill. I met with friends two or three times a week, and sometimes we played cards. I am not a good gambler, because I play to have fun and not to win; that meant I lost money all the time. Mom was not happy that I was gambling, but she always covered my losses.

In the evenings I joined the same friends at a café by the Dejla River, where we talked about our lives, played dominoes, drank tea, and snacked on Chinese green beans and bread with onions and tomatoes.

CHAPTER 15

Back Behind Bars, July 10, 1968

"Cold watermelon." Mom put the fruit plate on the end table next to my bed and left the room before I could say anything.

It was a lazy hot afternoon, one year to the day from my imprisonment the previous year. Mom was cooking dinner, expecting Dad to come home from work shortly. I lay on my bed with a book in my hands. Overwhelmed with thoughts, I laid the book on my chest and closed my eyes.

One year and one month had passed since my graduation. I spent two weeks imprisoned on a military base, then I worked for a couple of months. Now I was spending most of my days at home. In the evenings I met friends to pass the time. *What kind of life was this? Will I ever be able to live a normal and productive life?*

The doorbell rang and snapped me out of my reverie. Mom ran out of the kitchen, wiping her hands on her apron.

"Are you expecting someone?" she asked.

"No," I said, picking up my book again.

"It's *them* again," Mom said in a very low voice as she looked out of the bedroom window. I left the book on my bed and got up to open the door. Four men in plain clothes stood at our gate, a gray truck behind them.

Mom ran out to the gate with the letter she had from Captain Ahmad al-Azawi Abu al-Jibin, who had detained us the previous year, saying that he had found me and the others innocent of any crime.

"Is Yousuf here?" asked one of the men at the gate, the only one in a suit. "We would like to ask him a few questions," he added.

"Look," Mom showed him the letter. "They already interrogated him last year, and they released him because he did nothing."

"Let me see the letter, *ukhti* [my sister]," he said.

Mom handed the man the letter, confident he would read it and go away; after all, it was signed by a captain in the military intelligence. The man in the suit took the letter and tore it to pieces without even looking at it. Mom started bawling.

"Yousuf?" he asked, looking at me. I nodded my head. "Come with us," the man commanded.

"I am coming with him," Mom said.

"*Ukhti makoo haja* [My sister, there is no need]," the guy in the suit addressed her. "He will be back before sunset."

I opened the gate and walked out. Two men grabbed me by the arms and led me to the truck. To my surprise I saw Fouad Abu al Mator sitting in the back of the truck. Fouad looked at me, and his eyes said everything. *They* are not going to leave us alone.

As the truck started moving, I saw Mom despondent, bending to wipe her tears with her apron. Fouad and I glanced at one another. *Here we go again*, we thought. Last year we were lucky, *they* released us after two weeks. Are we going to survive this time?

The truck took us to the one-story Amn (national security) building, which looked more like a house than an office. The building faced a deserted street, avoided by everyone for fear of being stopped and questioned.

Fouad and I were taken directly to the back of the building and into one of the cells. The room was dark, dusty, and bare. A man lay on the floor, his head covered with a shirt. We sat quietly on the floor on the other side of the room. We could see and hear men in other cells through the barred walls.

"Did they tell you what they want from us?" I whispered to Fouad.

"No," he whispered back.

The man on the floor moved. He pulled the shirt off his head, exposing a bloodied face with one eye practically out of its socket. Our jaws dropped. We did not know what to do or say.

"What did you two do?" the man asked, squinting.

"We don't know," I answered. "Are you alright?"

The man smiled. "I will be alright by tomorrow when they come back for me." He spoke nonchalantly. "Why are you here?" he asked again.

"Because we are Jewish," I said. "Why did they do this to you?"

His face relaxed; he knew Jews were not a threat. "They did this to me because . . . I will not say what they want me to say," he said, then introduced himself.

His name was Omid. He was a Kurd, and he was imprisoned at Nigrat Al Salman (Al Salman Hole in the Ground) for five years because he was a member of the Communist party. Nigrat Al Salman was a notorious prison in the western desert, where political prisoners were held to isolate them. No one ever escaped that prison because it was a several days' walk from the nearest oasis in each direction.

Omid told us that every year he was brought to Baghdad and offered freedom in exchange for renouncing his membership in the party. Every year they beat him and tortured him, yet he refused to sign the disclaimer, so they sent him back to Nigrat Al Salman.

"Why don't you sign the disclaimer?" I asked. "Don't you think you can help the party more out of prison?"

"Maybe, but what will my children say? 'Our father had no spine?'" He shook his head. "I want to be an example for them; I want them to be proud of their father and to learn to be loyal to their beliefs." I admired the man and his courage. *I am not sure I could have done what he was doing,* I thought.

Every morning the guards took Omid, and they brought him back around noon limping and bloodied. But after an hour or so of rest, he would be up and in good spirits again.

My mother found out where we were being held and dropped off food for us at the front office every day. We shared our food with Omid, who shared everything he knew about the Amn in return. He told us that the building we were being held in was used for interrogations and torture, that all the prisoners were political, and that their stay there was for the short term. He told us about the idiosyncrasies of each one of the guards and how to deal with them. Most importantly, Omid advised us to go north to the Kurdish area when we were released. He told us that the Kurds were friendly with Israel and were trained by Israelis. He assured us that they would be helpful and would take us across the border to Iran.

On the fourth day, Omid did not come back to the cell. We never knew what his fate was. We hoped he was taken back to Nigrat Al Salman.

We started to think that they had forgotten about us. Five days went by, and no one asked for us or talked to us. Then on the sixth day, a guard took us to the front of the building, where a man dressed in a light-blue suit told us we were being moved to the central prison in Al-Adhamiyah, a suburb in northern Baghdad. The central prison was for long-term prisoners. We knew that due to a new law, Jews and Ba'athists could be imprisoned indefinitely without a hearing or court sentence. At the time, around forty-five Jews were being held in the central prison, some for as long as one year.

"Why are we being held?" I asked the man, who just shrugged. "What did we do?"

"My job is to arrange for the transportation, that's all I know," he replied.

The truck transporting the two of us stopped at the Shorja bazaar, where the driver went out to buy cigarettes. Fouad and I sat in the open back of the truck with a guard. I wondered if by chance Dad was around, since his *makhzan* was close by. I was sure if he knew I was in the area, he would run to the truck to talk to me. I would have loved to touch his hand and to tell him how much I loved him.

Around us, life went on as usual. Kids lined up in front of the ice-cream shop, a man sat at a small table at the juice store, men and women were having late lunches at the *shawarma* place, people stood in front of the newspaper shack, and a book salesman sat with his books spread on the sidewalk. I wondered, *Will I ever see this again?*

At the central prison we were given rolled-up mats and taken directly to our cell. As Fouad and I walked in, we were immediately surrounded by the Jewish detainees. I recognized most of them—well-known doctors, lawyers, accountants, and merchants. They were in pajamas and looked pale and anxious. They wanted to know why we were there and how life was outside of the prison walls.

When it came to where Fouad and I would place our mats, there was a big argument. No one wanted to move their mats to make space for us. Eventually, Mom's cousin Gurgi Shamash, who was among the prisoners, moved his mat and made space for the two of us. He told us that he had been there for eight months, and no one bothered to interrogate him or even talk to him.

"The guards treat us nicely because we tip them all the time," he said. "But it has been very tough, because everyone here is very tense."

On Wednesday, our third day in the central prison, everyone was more interested in what was taking place outside the prison walls. The guards told us that the Ba'ath party had staged a coup and seized power. Among the leaders of the coup, we heard the name Saddam Hussein, whom not many people had heard of at the time. His uncle, Ahmad Abu al-Bakr, led the July 17 coup, as it was known later.

The probable impact of this coup on us was the subject of discussion all day. One thing everyone agreed on was that based on the Ba'athists' previous actions and the laws they implemented when they were in power for eight months in 1963, matters would only get worse for all Iraqis, and especially for our Jewish community.

Friday, the weekly day off in Iraq, was visitation day. My mother came to see me and brought me clothes and food. She hugged me and would not let go.

"Mom, I am okay," I assured her.

We sat down in a corner of the prison's courtyard, where many other prisoners were meeting with their visitors. Tears ran down her cheeks.

"Your dad found someone who managed to put your and Fouad's *hajez* [indefinite imprisonment] papers on hold," Mom whispered as she looked around to make sure no one was listening. "They sent you here before the order came down because they needed the space at the Amn building," she said, smiling. "We will find a way to have the order canceled and get you two out of here."

"How are you and Baba doing?"

"We are doing well considering," Mom said. "How about you? How are they treating you?"

"We are being held with all the Jewish detainees in a large room," I answered. "The guards are helpful because of the big tips they get. I am keeping to myself; I read most of the time."

"Where do you get books from?" Mom asked.

"I borrow them from the other detainees."

"Are they nice to you?"

"All in all, yes. They are very anxious and nervous. . . . They argue about the smallest things," I added. "Your cousin Gurgi Shamash has been very good to us."

"Please say hello to him and see if he needs anything," Mom said. "What does everyone do all day?"

"They read, they play backgammon, they listen to the radio, and talk."

I think that Mom left that day calmer than she was when she came.

Three days after Mom's visit, a guard with a paper in his hand barged into the room. Everyone went quiet, not knowing what to expect.

"Yousuf Dabby and Fouad Yakub!" the guard shouted. "Collect your stuff and come with me, now."

"Where are you taking them?" one of the detainees asked.

"To the front office," the guard said.

"They must be taking you two to Qasr al-Nihaya [Palace of the End, called that because no one imprisoned there left alive]," another detainee said.

"Or maybe they will release them," said Gurgi.

"No way," someone else said, and everyone nodded in agreement.

We put our clothes into our duffel bags, gave our food and small items we had collected in jail to fellow detainees, said our goodbyes, and walked out of the large cell. At the door I stopped and turned to have a last look at the detainees, then waved as they wished us good luck.

At the front office they gave us each a sealed manila envelope.

"Your files are in the envelope," the clerk said. "You will be taken back to the Amn building." Then, with a strange smile, he looked at me and Fouad and said, "Good luck."

We climbed into the back of a truck, each deep in thought. *Now comes the real interrogation*, I thought.

The truck drove through Rasheed Street and past the Shorja bazaar, not stopping this time. We got off the truck and were led into the infamous building. We were seated on a wooden bench in the vestibule and left alone.

Seated by the front door with no guards watching us? That was strange. Men walked in and out of the building right by us, some looking at us with curiosity. Forty minutes later a man appeared at the end of the vestibule and signaled to us to follow him. He stopped at the first door in the hallway and knocked. The sign next to the door said "DIRECTOR."

"Come in," came the answer. It sounded like an order. The man opened the door and followed us into the room.

The director sat on a big chair behind an old executive desk facing the door. He wore a light-gray suit. To our right, a black couch sat under a window covered by sheers. Behind us was another smaller black couch. The director watched us walk in and stand in front of him.

"I have an intelligence report here that on Friday, May 10, this year you were driving along Qanat al-Jaish [the Army Canal] taking photos of the bridges," the director said, looking at us with a paper in his hand. Qanat al-Jaish was a man-made waterway to the east of Baghdad, constructed in 1959 to bring in irrigation and drinking water from the Tigris River to the area.

"I have never seen the canal," I said.

"Neither have I," said Fouad.

"We know you were not there," the director said, "but in order for me to release you, I need you to come up with an alibi, someone who will say you were with them that evening."

"Our parents?" I asked.

"That does not work!" the director said. "Think hard. . . ." Fouad and I looked at each other and then at the director.

"Amal can be your alibi," the director said.

Amal was my Christian girlfriend during the last two years in college. I had not seen her for at least a year. *Why is he bringing her into this? More importantly, why is he trying to help us?*

"Call her," the director said, pointing to the black phone on his desk. "Call her and ask her to come here."

Is he serious? I thought. *Even if I get a hold of Amal, why would she come here and get involved in this?*

"Tell her not to be scared," the director went on. "She will sign a statement, and the three of you will go home."

"I can't do that, *sayedi* [sir]," I said.

"Call her." He pointed to the phone on his desk again. "Tell her you need her to testify that she was with you that evening so we can release you two. Tell her she is the only person who can do that for you." Looking into my eyes, the director said, "You have my word, she will only be here for half an hour. We will not harm her." *How can I believe him?* I thought.

The director lifted the phone off its cradle and handed it to me. I looked at Fouad with the phone in my hand, and Fouad nodded. The director looked at his papers and dialed a number, and the phone started ringing. *He has Amal's phone number? He had obviously planned this, but why would he help us?* I wondered. *Does Amal know about this?*

Amal picked up the phone. "Hello."

"Hello, Amal," I mumbled in a shaky voice.

"Yousuf?" Amal was surprised. "Is that you? Where are you?"

"Listen, I am at the Amn building." I could hear her gasp. "I have been held here for a few days with Fouad Abu al Mator." I paused to let her absorb what I had said. "We are being held because someone claims they saw us taking photos of the bridges at Qanat al-Jaish. We need someone to testify under oath that they were with us on the evening of Friday, May 10, to prove our innocence. If you say we were together somewhere else, they will let us go," I said. "They assured me they won't keep you for more than one hour."

It's a big favor to ask, I thought. *I do not blame her if she says no. How can anyone trust these criminals?* She was quiet. *Please, say no,* I silently begged her.

"I will be there in fifteen," Amal said and hung up. I could not believe her courage. I was more scared for her than for myself.

"Go outside and wait for her," the director told me. Seeing my hesitation, he repeated, "Go!"

Fouad and I left the director's office. Fouad sat on the bench in the vestibule, and I walked out of the building. It was a beautiful day, relatively cool for July. There was not a soul around. *Is she really coming?* I wondered.

Amal and I had gotten closer in our junior year of college. We would meet at her home or mine to study together. Neither her parents nor mine approved, but we became very close. After I was released from prison the first time, we decided to stop seeing each other because it was not safe for her.

Soon, I saw Amal's baby-blue Volkswagen Beetle approach

the turnaround in front of the building and signaled to her. She parked her car and got out, her long, blond hair blowing in the light breeze. She wore a conservative, below-the-knee yellow dress, and a small yellow purse dangled from her shoulder.

"Thank you for coming. I love you, but you are crazy."

Amal smiled. We knew we were being watched. As we walked into the building, Fouad stood up to greet her and folded his hands to say thank you. As we walked into his office, the director stood up and asked Amal to sit down in front of his desk.

"Were Yousuf and Fouad with you the evening of Friday, May 10?"

"Yes," Amal said without hesitation.

The director smiled. He handed Amal a sheet of paper and a pen.

"Write," he said. Amal wrote as he dictated. "On this date, today, July 23, 1968, I testify under oath that on the evening of Friday, May 10, 1968, I met Yousuf Dabby and Fouad Haskel for coffee at the Dejla Café. We were there from 4:00 p.m. to 7:00 p.m." He paused. "Write your name and sign."

The director took the paper, reviewed it, and seemed relieved. He looked as if a heavy weight had been taken off his shoulders.

"Thank you, Miss." He looked at Fouad and me. "You are free to go now."

Dad must have arranged for our release just like Mom said, I thought. *The director brought Amal in because she would be a safe alibi.*

"Did it occur to you," I asked Amal a few minutes later as we drove off in her car, "that this may have been a trap, and that you could have been accused of being a spy?"

"Of course, that was the first thing that came to my mind," Amal said, smiling. "But I would never forgive myself if I didn't help when you needed me."

A few days later Mom visited Amal at her home to say thank you. She met her mom for the first time. I cannot imagine what ran through the minds of Amal's parents when they found out that their daughter had gone into the lion's den to help me.

The next time I saw Amal was thirty years later. She and her ten-year-old son were visiting a cousin of hers in Los Angeles, trying to get U.S. papers for her family. She and her family had left Iraq for Jordan, where her husband was waiting with their two other kids. I tried to help but could not do much. Eventually, she and her family emigrated to a Western country. I still feel bad that I could not return her favor.

CHAPTER 16
No Light at the End of the Tunnel, 1969

Following the 1968 coup, the Ba'ath regime in Iraq was very weak and was in constant fear of being the target of another coup. In November 1968, to terrorize the population, the regime announced that it had discovered a spy ring that they claimed was working to destabilize Iraq. Seventeen Jews from Baghdad and Basra were arrested. Among them was Jacob Atraghji, Yvette's first cousin, a father of seven. He was transferred from Basra to Qasr Al-Nihaya, near Baghdad, where he was tortured and murdered in front of the others to get them to sign false confessions. His family was told that he ran away from prison. It was not until two years later that his wife, Tina, was told what really happened by a prisoner who had witnessed his torture and death.

A mock trial was held for twelve Jews, three Muslims, and two Christians. The proceedings were shown on television every evening. On the night of January 26, 1969, I stayed up late to hear the court verdict. Fourteen of the alleged spies were convicted

Tahrir Square, Baghdad, January 27, 1969.

and condemned to death by hanging, among them nine Jews. The other three were sentenced to prison for different times.

The men were executed immediately after the verdict was read, and in the morning their corpses were hung in Al-Tahrir (Independence) Square in the center of Baghdad. Placards draped the hanging bodies listing the name, date of birth, and the city where they came from. On the bodies of the Jews the word "JEW" was written in red. Radio Baghdad invited the citizens to "come and enjoy the feast."

That day, Saturday January 27, 1969, was a dark and dreadful day. Around one million people flocked to Al-Tahrir Square to celebrate the hangings. We stayed home and watched on television with horror as people danced and picnicked around the hanging bodies. The remaining Jewish prisoners, except for two, were executed in August of the same year, and their bodies were hung in public squares.

Following the January hangings, Iraq faced an international outrage. Many Western journalists, mostly Americans, flocked to Baghdad to investigate. The government took them to interview the chief rabbi, Hakham Sasson Khadouri, who denied that the Jewish community was being persecuted or mistreated. He had no choice because his only son was being held in prison.

The journalists were taken to Frank Iny School, the only operational Jewish school in Baghdad at the time, to prove to the world that the Jews enjoyed their freedom and had their own educational system. Mike Wallace of *60 Minutes* was one of the journalists who toured the school. The children in the school snuck notes into the journalists' pockets. The notes were cries for help and were very effective in getting the truth out.

The world reacted with anger. We were excited to hear news reports about our condition on the BBC and Voice of America radio stations. We felt that finally our cries had been heard, and the world would come to our help.

As an appeasement, the Iraqi government announced that it would allow Jews to leave the country with one caveat: They would lose their Iraqi citizenship. Almost the whole community ran to apply for passports.

In the meantime, the Ba'ath regime continued with the mock trials and falsely accused those who opposed the regime of being Zionist and American spies by associating them with Jews. The alleged spies were hanged and their bodies were hung in public squares in different cities to scare the people and strengthen the government's hold on the country. By the end of August 1969, fifty-one Jews had been murdered, hundreds of Jews were imprisoned, and many more had vanished. The rampage of the Ba'ath regime against the Jews never stopped.

The Jewish community's situation worsened by the day. There was no light at the end of the tunnel. Beginning in August 1969, a few courageous Jews started finding their way to the eastern border and escaping to Iran. Soon, more people followed. Some were apprehended by the authorities and were brought back to Baghdad, imprisoned, their belongings confiscated, and then released. It was rumored that the government turned the other way purposely to allow the Jews to leave the country.

One hot afternoon in July 1969, Mom and I were sitting on our front porch. I was reading, and Mom was sewing. I noticed a man looking in through our garden gate. I got up to see what or who he was looking for.

"I am looking for . . . Yousuf," he read from a notebook in his hand. "Are you Yousuf?" I nodded. "You are ordered to be at the Ministry of Defense tomorrow morning at ten." He handed me a piece of paper. "Show this letter to the guard at the gate of the ministry." It was like déjà vu.

"Do you understand?" He looked into my eyes, and I nodded again.

"Why? What did he do?" Mom came to the gate and asked.

"The Mukhabarat [intelligence service] wants to talk to him. They want confirmation that Ahmad al-Azawi Abu al-Jibin took bribes to release Yousuf and the others two years ago," the man said. "Abu al-Jibin is being interrogated. Your son's testimony will be helpful."

He turned around, climbed into a jeep, and drove off. I could hear my heartbeat. I knew that people taken to the Ministry of Defense often disappeared without a trace.

I heard Mom sniffling. I turned around and she hugged me. "They won't leave you alone," she said. I could see that she was very anxious.

Because phone lines had been cut off at Jewish homes and businesses after the Six-Day War in 1967, we had no phone at home, so Mom spent the rest of the day traveling by bus from home to home. First, she reached out to Mr. Samra, who had been Abu al-Jibin's messenger two years before. Mr. Samra panicked and begged Mom never to admit to bribing Abu al-Jibin. Then she went to Jack's house—Jack had been imprisoned with me—to get his mother's opinion. The two women agreed that the right thing would be to not admit to bribery.

That evening the mother of Albert, who was also imprisoned with me two years before, came to our house.

"The kids have to tell the truth," she said forcefully. "We had to bribe Abu al-Jibin to get him to release our kids, didn't we? Let him meet his fate."

"But that would mean our kids did something wrong and we bribed him to release them. We will all be in trouble." Mom tried to dissuade Albert's mother, who was adamant.

"Mark my words," she said, looking at the ground. "They will torture your son, even kill him. They will do the same to the rest of the group until one of them says what they need, to incriminate Abu al-Jibin." Both women started crying.

At breakfast in the morning, Dad was very quiet. I studied his face. I wanted to remember him at that moment. I got up and kissed his head.

When Mom and I walked out the door, I stopped and turned around.

"Did you forget something?" Mom asked.

"No, I just want to see our home one more time."

"Come on, Yousuf, you are coming back with me. Do you really think I will leave you in their hands?"

The Ministry of Defense sat on a huge parcel of land bounded by Rasheed Street on one side and by the Dejla River on the other. At the gate of the ministry, my name was on the list. Mom and I were driven in a jeep to the main building by the river. We walked in, and the soldier at the reception desk invited us to sit down and offered us hot tea.

Mom and I were quiet. My brain was racing. I did not know what to expect. *Would I see Abu al-Jibin? Was he being tortured? Would they believe me when I said we did not give him any money to release us? Would they torture me? How much torture could I handle? Should I just tell them the truth?*

One hour went by. Then a man in a gray suit came in the room and headed toward us. Mom and I stood up.

"Thank you, Yousuf, for coming here and for your patience," he said. "You can go home now, we don't need you anymore." Seeing the surprise on our faces he added, "Abu al-Jibin had a heart attack and died last night during his interrogation."

I did not know what to do or say. Mom quickly extended her arm to shake the man's hand.

"Thank you, *sayedi* [sir], *ma'al salama* [we leave you with peace]."

The officer walked us out of the building and ordered the jeep driver to take us to the entrance gate. In the jeep, Mom put her hands on mine. She could not hide her happiness. I could not hide my confusion.

CHAPTER 17

Mom's Ultimatum

As the government continued its wave of terror against the Jews, we lived in fear. Jewish men were taken at random, imprisoned, and tortured. Few came out of prison alive. Three Jewish homes were invaded and whole families were murdered. Public hangings of alleged spies continued. Uncle Khadouri was taken and tortured a couple of times and was only released after big bribes were paid.

We were having tea in our family room one afternoon when Dad surprised us.

"Yousuf, you have to leave. We have to find a way to get you out," he said. Mom's jaw dropped, but Dad continued. "*They* will come for you again sooner than later, and this time we may not be able to help you." He put his tea glass on the side table and looked at me.

"Baba, I am not leaving without you and Mama," I retorted. "You know I could have left with my friends when I graduated high school, but I did not, and you know why." Dad nodded. "If I go, you will never leave." I got up and sat next to him on the couch. "Why can't we all leave together?"

"I will not leave illegally," Dad said. "I am too old to be caught and imprisoned."

"Apply for a passport then," I said.

The government, pressured by the international community, announced that Jews could travel out of Iraq and that applications for passports would be considered. Rumors were that they would allow older people to leave. "There is a good chance that you and Mom will get a passport."

"And where do you suggest we go?" Dad said. "We don't read or write, and the only language we can speak is Arabic."

"You can go to Holland. Our friends who escaped recently are there already, and they will help you."

"And leave you here?" Dad asked. "You must be out of your mind."

"Baba, I will follow you. Wait for me in Holland. If I don't make it, you can still come back."

"That's very easy for you to say," Dad said.

Mom finally joined the conversation. "Abu Saleh, listen to your son. What are we doing here? What kind of a life is this? What if they take you next?" Mom paused. "Yousuf is right, it is time to leave."

Dad was deep in thought. We left it at that.

I was very excited and did not wait; that evening I joined my friends in their discreet search for a smuggler to take us across the border.

The next morning, Mom said at breakfast, "We can't go."

"Why? What happened? I thought we agreed yesterday," I said. "You and Baba will leave when you get your passports, and I will follow you."

Dad stopped eating and looked at Mom.

"I don't want you to end up like your brother, Saleh," Mom said, "marrying late in life and to a non-Jew." Mom and Dad were not happy that Saleh had married out of the faith; intermarriage was not accepted in our community.

"Mama . . . for God's sake."

"I want to see you married before we leave."

I almost said, *So do I, and I have just the right girl.*

"Oh my God, Mama," I said. "I will get married when I find the right girl, and you will be there to approve."

"No, I want to see you marry a girl from a family we know, someone from our background," Mom said. "And the sooner, the better."

I agree with you, I thought.

"How?" I asked. "Who is in that state of mind now?"

"Look around," Mom said. "Choose your life partner from our community."

"Baba, say something," I pleaded.

Dad remained quiet. I think he agreed with Mom.

"I am not leaving until I see you married," Mom asserted. "That's it."

Of course, I did not take Mom's ultimatum seriously. I was in love with Yvette, and my dream was to spend the rest of my life with her. It was a dream because of all that was going on at the time. Moreover, I lived with my parents, had no job, and I could be imprisoned again at any time. Mom's ultimatum, however, made me think, *Why not move on with my life and not lose the girl I love? We can start living our lives together—and escape together, if she is okay with that.*

CHAPTER 18

Yvette

I had known Yvette all my life. Our families were friends, and our fathers did business together. She was the third of four children born to Asher Atraghji and Farha Cohen: Rachel, Rosy, Yvette, and Ezra. Her sister Rachel left for Canada in 1963 and from there she went to Israel.

Yvette was one year behind me in school and at Al-Hikma University. She was beautiful and smart, and I admired her. After graduation, we went out a few times for coffee with her sister Rosy and her boyfriend, Albert, and I fell in love with her.

We continued to see each other during the horrible years when I was imprisoned twice and her cousin Jacob was murdered in prison. She knew that I loved her, but I never had the courage to tell her that because of the times.

I cannot forget the afternoon we went to the driver testing grounds so that Yvette and Rosy could practice for their driver's license test. I taught them both to drive in my baby-blue 1965 Fiat 1500 with standard transmission and light-gray leather

Yvette.

seats. In 1970, to prepare them for the driver's test, I drove them and Albert to the testing grounds, a dirt lot next to the one-story building of the Department of Motor Vehicles. In the middle of the lot stood several empty oil barrels. Some of the barrels formed two circles, while the ones surrounding the circles formed a figure eight. To pass the driver's test, one had to drive the car backward around the two circles within the figure eight without the car touching any of the barrels.

After showing them what to do, I got out and gave the driver's seat to Yvette. It was just before sunset on a warm summer day. The sky was orange and blue, and it felt muggy. Yvette moved her head to the side and pushed her long black hair away from her face. She started the car, put the gear in reverse,

With Yvette, Rosy, and Albert, 1971.

and took her foot off the clutch. The car jumped backward, the tires spun, and brown clouds of dust rose in the air.

"Stop, stop!" I screamed.

Albert jumped out of the car, but Rosy stayed in the back seat, holding on to the front one. The car headed toward a barrel. I ran to move the barrel before the car hit it. As the car turned, Albert ran to move another barrel out of the way. Albert's prescription glasses fell to the ground, and he cussed. I was sweating bullets as I was pushing against the car, trying to stop it from hitting a barrel. My shiny car got all dusty. *Thank God no one is here,* I told myself, *this would be a very entertaining show.*

Albert and I ran from one barrel to the next, pushing them away from the moving car. We were breathing pure dust. In the back seat, Rosy's reddish curly hair moved back and forth with the movement of the car. In no time Albert and I had managed to distort the precisely arranged figure; now it looked more like an amoeba.

"Let's come back tomorrow. I can't do this anymore," I said.

Albert and I stood outside the car with beads of sweat running down our foreheads. When our eyes met, Yvette smiled. She was beautiful, and I loved her.

In October of 1970, I told Yvette that I loved her and proposed to her. She was happy and said yes. I went home that evening and told Mom; she was very excited and immediately asked Aunt Simha to go to Yvette's parents to ask for Yvette's hand. A few days later the whole Atraghji family came to our home and told my parents they approved, and together they scheduled our engagement to be on Saturday, November 7, 1970.

When I announced my engagement to my domino buddies at the café, a loud discussion erupted.

Yvette and family, 1962. Standing: Yvette, Rachel, Rosy, and Ezra. Sitting: Farha and Asher.

"Why would you get engaged now?"

"How can you marry her? Have you even kissed her?"

"Do you really want to get married here?"

"But we will leave and start our life somewhere else," I said.

"What if you won't be able to leave? How will you provide?"

"Wouldn't it be wiser to wait till you are both out?"

I could not disagree with my friends; it was crazy to commit at a time like this, but nothing could dissuade me. I loved Yvette. I had found the woman I wanted to spend the rest of my life with, and I was not going to let her go.

Just as we were preparing for the engagement party, a big surprise came. Early one morning our doorbell rang. It was Hussein, Uncle Khadouri's chauffeur. He was in a state of shock and could not contain himself.

"The house is empty," he said. "Nobody is there. Where is everyone?" Hussein recounted that he came to work as he did every morning, took the car out of the garage, and waited for Uncle Khadouri. When Uncle did not come out of the house, Hussein rang the doorbell to check on him. No one answered. Hussein went around the house and peeked through the windows. The house looked deserted.

That was how we found out that Uncle Khadouri and his family had escaped. We didn't find out how until much later when my parents met them in Israel. Uncle Khadouri left with Aunt Simha; their two sons, Joseph and Jack; and their youngest daughter, Farah (Kathy), her husband, Sabah, and Farah's mother-in-law. They left with two of Uncle Khadouri's business partners and their families. Dressed up like Kurds, they traveled by cars north to the Kurdish area and into Iran with the help of the Kurds.

Dad was upset that his brother had left the country and did not take us with him. Moreover, he did not even tell him. But Dad's love for his brother was stronger than anyone could know, and this didn't affect their relationship.

"Take the car back, leave it in the garage, and go home," Dad told Hussein. "They must have escaped, and you should not be there when the authorities find out."

It was a very anxious time. Every day we woke up to the news that a community member or family had left. All the community talked about was leaving the country, and everyone was scrambling to find out how to do it.

Rosy was offered the chance to escape with some of her friends. Out of an abundance of caution, they did not want to pick her up from her home. Rosy and Yvette went for a walk along Abu Nawas Street, along the Dejla River. Rosy carried a small duffel bag with one change of clothes. Her friends picked her up in their car and drove north. They hid in a Kurdish home for a couple of days before they were taken across the border into Iran.

"Who will be here to attend our engagement party?" asked Yvette jokingly.

The party was held at Yvette's parents' house. It was a happy event in a turbulent time. All our friends and family who had not left the country by then showed up, including my disapproving domino buddies. All everyone talked about was who had escaped and how they did it.

Hakham Daweed recited the *kiddush* and read the *brachot* (blessings). In Iraq, the custom was to recite the first set of blessings of the wedding at the engagement ceremony and the second set at the wedding ceremony. That meant a breakup after the engagement was considered a divorce. We exchanged gold coins, and I stepped on a glass to break it, reinforcing our commitment.

That night Yvette and I kissed for the first time.

Our engagement, November 7, 1970.

With our parents at our engagement.

CHAPTER 19

A Wedding and a Tearful Goodbye, 1970

"My cousin Olivia and her father are leaving today," Yvette told me. "The same people will take us across the border."

"When?"

"We can go in five days."

"Wow, that is great," I said. In fact, I could have left at a moment's notice; I had no job and no one to report to. However, my parents had not yet received their passports, so I would be leaving them behind. *I have to talk to Mom and Dad,* I thought. *They will have to assure me that they will follow us as soon as possible.*

When I went home and told my parents about the opportunity to leave, they were very happy.

"It is for the best," Dad said. "Now I can leave this place not worried about leaving you behind."

"But Baba, how are you two going to leave? What if you don't get passports?"

"Son, do not worry, they started issuing passports to older people," Dad said. "Everyone thinks that Canada has paid Iraq lots of money to let the Jews leave."

"We will follow you as soon as we get our passports," Mom said.

Yvette told me that her father wanted to talk to us, so we went to her home in the evening. Yvette and I sat on one side of the room. Across from us sat Yvette's father, Asher, his brother Gurgi, and their wives, Farha and Marcelle. *Asher and his brother must have something important to tell us,* I thought. The two men had just come home from work and were still in suits and ties.

"Are you planning to leave soon?" Asher asked.

"*Inshallah* [God willing]," I said, looking at Yvette.

"Son, where are you two planning to live when you leave?" Gurgi asked.

"Israel," I responded with no hesitation.

There was a pause; you could have heard a pin drop.

"We will give you 2,000 dinars [around $5,000] to start your life," Asher announced, and Gurgi nodded in agreement.

"Thank you so much," I said. "I hope you will join us soon."

"But you can't take our daughter and leave just like that," said Gurgi, who had been fidgeting in his seat. "You two have to get married before you leave."

Gurgi was the youngest and toughest of Yvette's five uncles. Without half his teeth, his face sagged. I looked at Yvette. *Another ultimatum,* I thought.

"But Uncle, we are planning to leave in four days," I said.

"*Ibni,* if you two want to leave the country, you must get married first," Asher said.

There was no room for discussion. Yvette and I looked at each other. We were at a loss. *What are we to do?*

"We can do it," Yvette's mother, Farha, jumped in. "Four days is plenty of time to plan the wedding."

In the next three days, Farha and Mom were very busy. Farha found a wedding dress for Yvette and fitted her. A three-layer wedding cake was purchased. The flower girls were chosen. Yvette's brother went around on his bike announcing the date of our wedding ceremony. No invitations were printed; the whole community was invited. Our wedding day, December 7, 1970, fell on the same date my parents were married thirty-seven years before. *What a coincidence,* I thought.

Two days before the wedding Yvette's parents hosted the traditional *leilat al-Hinni* (henna night), a Middle Eastern custom where the families and close friends of the bride and the groom celebrate the upcoming wedding with fun songs. One song preformed in Jewish dialect describes how the mother of the bride dazzled and captivated the groom: *Afaki Afaki ashlon qene'eteno wa akhethtenou.* ("Well done, well done how you convinced him and took him.") The highlight of the evening is when family members take turns and place henna around the fingertips of both the bride and the groom.

The evening of our wedding, Abe, a close friend, picked us and the flower girls up in a 1968 Chrysler Newport. Yvette's white lace wedding dress with long sleeves was beautiful. I had a dark suit on, and the flower girls were all dressed in white lace dresses. We went first to Nerso Studio, a well-known photographer, for wedding photos. Then we went to the synagogue. As we walked down the driveway to the side door of the synagogue, we could hear the din inside the big sanctuary.

Mom was waiting at the side door of the synagogue, and when she saw us she started ululating. She threw a clay pot on the floor, breaking it, to ward off the evil eye. Asher was waiting inside the synagogue. The flower girls took their positions, and Asher held Yvette's right arm and started walking her down the aisle. Mom and I went up to the stage to join my father, Yvette's mother, and other family members. More than three hundred people filled the benches on both sides of the aisle, all dressed in their best, looking happy. The chief rabbi, Hakham Sasson Khadouri, sat in the front row in his traditional garb. On another front bench sat Hakham Daweed (David). It's hard to believe, but the only two rabbis in our small community were not on speaking terms because of a previous disagreement.

As the bridal party approached the stage, I went down to take Yvette from her father. I held her left arm, and we went back up on the stage. Surrounded by our parents, close relatives, and the cantor , we stood facing the invitees. For a moment it seemed that time had stopped, and nothing outside the synagogue mattered. My parents and Yvette's parents could not stop smiling; their happiness was contagious.

Mr. Paniri, the cantor, recited the seven *brachot*. Yvette and I drank a sip of wine each, exchanged rings, and I stepped on the glass and broke it. The room erupted in ululations and applause. I felt my hands trembling and sweat running down my forehead. Suddenly I felt anxious. *What if something goes wrong and we cannot leave tomorrow?*

Our wedding, December 7, 1970.
Bottom: Linda, the flower girl, carrying the bridal train.

Our wedding.

Our ketubah, written December 7, 1970.

As we walked down from the stage, people ran to greet us.

"Please tell my son when you see him that we are okay," one lady told me.

"Look for my children. We haven't heard from them since they left three months ago," an old man whispered in my ear.

Because of the surprise wedding, everyone figured out that we must have planned to leave, and everyone wanted to send messages to their loved ones. *Will I remember their messages?* I thought. *And more importantly, will I be able to deliver them?*

We drove to our home, where Mom had invited close friends to dinner. People filled the living and family rooms. Drinks and mezes were served. The table in the dining room was covered with all kinds of traditional food. The chefs Mom hired had been cooking for two days.

Farha walked up to us. "It's a no-go," she whispered to Yvette and me. "We just got a note from Olivia's father. He wrote: 'The delivery of the baby was very difficult' and suggested we use a different doctor." The news, like cold water, dampened our joy. Mom was watching us from across the room, and she knew what had just happened.

No one said anything. The party went on. When the guests left, they said their goodbyes to us and wished us the best in our coming adventure. Our parents joined us in the living room. Yvette and I looked at each other. *What do we do now? How long will it be before we can leave? Where do we stay now?*

"Do not worry," Mom said, seeing the anxiety on our faces. "Remember: As one door closes, many other doors open."

I hope she is right, I thought.

Yvette and I spent that night at Baghdad Hotel, the fanciest and most modern hotel in town. It was located on Abu Nawas Street, and every one of its rooms had a view of the Dejla River.

In the morning we left the hotel and drove down Abu Nawas to a popular fisherman's kiosk to purchase a *masgouf*, a popular Iraqi dish reserved for special occasions. *Masgouf* is made with a freshwater fish, *shaboot,* found only in the Dejla and barbecued in a special way.

I walked down to the edge of the river with the fisherman, where he pulled out a rope with several live fish hanging on it, each on its own little hook. I looked at the fish flapping in the air, trying to breath out of water, and saw myself and my community. Like these fish, we were struggling to stay alive while, one by one, we were picked to be killed.

"Which one would you like?" the fisherman asked. He pointed to a fish. "How about this one?"

I nodded. The fisherman took the fish he chose off the main rope and walked back to the kiosk with me. The fish was shaking violently and struggling to stay alive.

He put the fish on the metal table, then clubbed it on its head with the wooden handle of a big sharp knife. The fish died instantly. After scaling and gutting it, he split it lengthwise down the back, washed it, and splayed it flat. He seasoned the inside with olive oil and salt. Next to his table, a wood fire burned in a mound on the ground. The fisherman impaled the fish with two wooden sticks and stood it with its belly facing the fire. Fifteen minutes later he took the fish off the sticks and laid it flat with the skin on the charcoal for a few minutes before he put it on a large tray. He garnished it with sliced tomatoes, grilled onions, parsley, and *amba* and covered it with a large, crispy flatbread straight out of the *tanoor* (clay oven). We took the tray home, where we had lunch with my parents.

I was anxious about our next move, and I am sure Yvette was too, but we did not talk about it. Had things gone as planned, we would have been on our way to freedom and to a new life. It never occurred to us that we would start our life in Baghdad. *We can live with my parents for now. But will we ever get another opportunity to leave?* I asked myself.

A few weeks after our wedding, Ezra and his cousins Rony and David (Tina's sons) escaped to Iran. Theirs was a difficult journey, and they had to walk through snow for days to cross the border.

My focus turned to helping my parents leave the country. Time went by slowly, and seven months later, on Sunday, June 6, 1971, my parents' passports were finally issued. Now they needed an entry visa from a country before they could leave Iraq. I went to the U.S. consulate to apply for a visa. I thought the visa would be granted without any problem since my brother was an American citizen. I was wrong.

"Your parents will stay in the States," the consul said. "They will not come back."

"They will not stay in the States, I promise," I said. "They just need a place to transit through to Israel, where they plan to join their two daughters. Please help them leave Iraq, please save them."

The U.S. consul did not believe me, nor did the consuls of Britain, France, and Italy. Exasperated and without much hope, I walked into the Dutch consulate. The girl at the front desk recognized me. She had been a fellow student at Al-Hikma University. I was sure she heard that I had been imprisoned and accused of spying for the Jesuits. I could see it in the way she was looking at me. I wanted to turn around and walk out, but it was too late.

The girl took the passports and the visa applications and went into the office behind her. Within minutes, she came out empty-handed. *What a waste of time,* I thought. *Here comes another denial.*

"The consul wants to see you," she said.

Oh my God, now for sure she thinks I am a spy. I followed her into the consul's office. The Dutch consul stood up behind the desk to greet me and asked me to sit across the desk from him. He was in his midforties, tall and blond, with blue eyes and a fair complexion.

"I will grant your parents the entry visa." His words engulfed me and quickened my heartbeat. "Tell your parents that they can stay in Holland if they want to—we will take care of them."

I did not have the time to digest what I heard before he continued.

"Tell your community that Holland will issue visas to help anyone who wants to leave Iraq, and they are welcome to stay in Holland." He took a deep breath and continued. "If you manage to leave the country and you need help, go to the Dutch consulate anywhere in the world. They will help you financially and grant you a visa."

I thanked him profusely. I walked out of the consulate in a daze, the stamped passports in my pocket. I still could not absorb everything I had heard. This was a godsend. I could not wait to give my parents the good news. On the way home it occurred to me that the girl at the consulate might report my visit to the police. Cold sweat broke out on my forehead.

At home, my parents were not exactly elated.

"What good is the visa?" my father asked. "You think your mom and I will go to Holland and leave you and Yvette here?"

"But Baba, we have talked about that. We will find a way to leave too."

"No, *ibni*, you escape first; we will not go before you leave." Dad sat down. He looked old and exhausted. Mom stood next to him.

"Your dad is right," she said. "We will not leave before you. We will blame ourselves if something happens to you."

That evening, after a lot of convincing, we made a deal. My parents would leave for Holland, where Rosy and Albert settled and could help them. To be on the safe side, Yvette and I would move to an apartment before my parents' departure. If we could not get out of the country in two months or if something went wrong, my parents would return. I did not think they could return, but it was the only way to convince them to leave.

On June 21, 1971, Yvette and I accompanied my parents to Baghdad Airport.

"Write every day," Mom said with tears running down her cheeks. Dad stood next to his suitcase nodding, his eyes red and teary.

"Mama, do not worry, we will be with you as soon as possible. You take care of yourself and Baba," I said. "Rosy and Albert will be waiting for you at the airport in Amsterdam."

We hugged and hugged, not wanting to let go. Yvette and I watched them as they walked toward the immigration kiosk. I felt as if a part of me was leaving. My eyes were dry, but I was crying inside. I wondered, *Am I ever going to see them again?*

The day Dad was afraid of had arrived. They were in their sixties and spoke no other language besides their native tongue, Arabic. They would be dependent on others. Dad gave $25,000 to a banker, who assured him that the money would be deposited in a bank in Switzerland in Dad's name. That was all Dad could get his hands on.

My parents left their home, the country where our ancestors had lived for over 2,500 years, with nothing but memories and perhaps $25,000. They left behind everything they had worked hard for, and at an old age they had to start a new life. I kept thinking that the world was really unfair to my parents and others like them. Young people can adjust and thrive if they move to foreign lands. But for my parents' generation, to be uprooted like that was brutal.

CHAPTER 20

Leaving Baghdad

I ran into the apartment. "Yvette, the cab is here," I yelled.

I saw Yvette standing in the middle of the living room, absorbing her surroundings with a small brown duffel bag in her hand.

"Come on, we have to go. . . ." I glanced at the calendar on the wall: July 27, 1971.

It's twenty-seven again, I thought. *The numbers two and seven have always been my lucky numbers. I was born on the 27th, and Yvette was born on the second; we were engaged on the seventh and married on the seventh. This is going to be a good day.*

"Give me a minute to say goodbye." Yvette interrupted my thoughts in a very solemn voice. I looked around. *What is she saying goodbye to?* We both knew when we moved in one month before that this apartment would be a temporary home for us. The furniture was scant, and the walls were left naked intentionally.

"It's not the apartment I am saying goodbye to. . . . This is goodbye to our whole life here, our family and friends." She started tearing up, but I was not going to let that slow us down. The moment we had planned for was here. I took the duffel bag from her hand and started toward the door. I heard her following me.

"My neck is really stiff, and I already have a headache," she said as we were going down the stairs to the street. "I don't know if I can keep this stuff around my neck for too long."

"Let's talk about that at your parents'."

We were leaving home for good with one change of clothing and "this stuff": a heavy gold necklace that Yvette had around her neck. When we got married seven months before, wedding gifts came in the form of money or gold coins. People gave us gifts that were easy to carry. Yvette got a dozen solid gold British pound coins. At her mother's suggestion, she had them mounted on a thick gold chain that she could wear around her neck under her shirt.

In the cab, I looked out the window, constructing a detailed photographic memory of the jaywalkers and cars fighting to claim the street, the lush green squares with children running around, and the neglected buildings with the paint peeling off. *This may be the last time we ever see this*, I thought. We were leaving Baghdad, where we were born and grew up, fell in love, and got married. We were leaving with nothing but memories—mostly painful—yet I felt part of me wanted to stay.

The cars honking brought me back to reality. This was the fourth time that week that we left the apartment with the brown duffel bag and took a cab to Yvette's parents' home. We had not used our car all week. We knew we were being watched and wanted to establish a routine that did not look suspicious. It worked; no one had followed us the day before, and no one was following us today.

I checked my jacket pocket. Our ID cards were there, two yellow cards with our photos and the word *Moussawi* (followers of Moses) scribbled in red above the photos. I hoped we would not be asked to show them—that would be the end.

It was around 5:00 p.m., a typical evening in Baghdad. Cars were racing each other, their drivers honking and shouting, and more people were in the street than on the sidewalk.

"I am going to miss that," I whispered to Yvette.

It wasn't us who chose which day of the week to escape. On the previous Friday, we were visiting Yvette's parents, and Asher told us, "I would like to see you tomorrow."

My heart dropped. "Why? Is anything wrong?" I asked.

"I have something to discuss with you in private."

On Saturday we drove to Yvette's parents' home. Farha opened the door smiling and saw that we were really worried.

"Don't worry, Asher is doing well," she said before either one of us could utter a word. "He just wanted to be cautious and talk to you in private."

She ushered us into the dining room, where Asher was having his daily Turkish coffee, away from all the action in the house, and closed the door behind us. We sat on the brown upholstered chairs across from Asher. Asher was in his seventies, tall, handsome, blond, blue-eyed, and lightly tanned. He was a listener and spoke very little, but not on that evening.

"Naeem came to my office two days ago," Asher started. "He claims that he has a contact who can smuggle you across the border into Iran." He pushed his coffee cup away and leaned on his elbows on the dinner table. "He told me that his contact would meet you in Erbil." Erbil is a Kurdish town 250 miles north of Baghdad.

Yvette and I were quiet. Asher looked at us intensely and continued. "I don't know whether I can believe Naeem."

"Why wouldn't you believe Naeem?" I asked sarcastically. Naeem was my father's partner and was not known for his truthfulness.

Asher ignored my sarcasm. "Naeem wants 750 dinars per person," he said.

I almost jumped up from my seat. "Seven hundred and fifty dinars per person! We can't afford that." That amount was equal to the median annual income of a worker at the time.

Asher leaned back in his seat. "I will pay the 1,500 dinars, that's not the problem. I'm more worried about your safety."

Farha brought in a tray with four steaming tea glasses and a plate of biscuits. "I don't like this plan," she said as she put the tray on the dinner table in front of us. "Are you guys crazy? Jumping in the fire . . ."

"*Amma* [Auntie], every day we stay here, we are in danger." I emphasized every word. "Did you forget that I have been imprisoned twice in the last three years, and it was by bribe and miracle that I got out?" I stopped to take a breath. "Last year *they* wanted me to testify against one of them; it was only by sheer luck that I did not have to do that. There is no end—sooner or later *they* will come for me again. We have to take our chances."

Farha sat down deep in thought. *I think she understands,* I thought. *Capture, imprisonment, or even death paled in comparison to our desire for a life free of fear. We really had nothing to lose.*

Asher and Farha looked at each other, then Asher turned to us. "*Awladi* [My children], I will not stop you." He exhaled and shook his head. "I want nothing more than to see you both out of here, *Allah wiyakem* [God be with you]."

Silence fell on the room as we sipped our tea.

"You want to do it, right?" I looked at Yvette, who had been very quiet.

"We have no choice," Yvette said, looking at her parents. "You know how frightening a knock on the door is to us, you know that every night we fool ourselves and turn off the doorbell so that we can sleep without worrying." She took a deep breath. "We can't miss this chance. . . . We have no choice."

Farha dropped her head. Asher broke the silence.

"It's settled then. Naeem told me that his contact, Saeed, will meet you outside the Erbil train station Wednesday morning."

"We will take the train to Erbil Tuesday night then," I said.

Asher's legs started shaking like they always did when he got nervous. He leaned forward, and almost whispering, he said, "I told Naeem that Tina and her children and David will be going with you."

Tina, Yvette's first cousin, grew up in Basra, a city 330 miles south of Baghdad. At a very young age, she married her first cousin Jacob, who worked in the family business. Tina and Jacob had seven children—six boys and Linda. In November 1968, a few months after Saddam Hussein rose to power, a wave of arrests and public hangings shook every city in Iraq. Jacob and sixteen other Jewish men were apprehended and accused of spying for Israel. Jacob was tortured and killed in front of the other detainees to make them sign confessions. His body was never returned to the family. Local newspapers reported that he had fled from prison and could not be found. Jacob was in his midforties.

Devastated, Tina moved to Yvette's parents' house in Baghdad to try to find the whereabouts of her husband. In 1970 the three older boys made their way out of Iraq. I cannot imagine what Tina's life was like, a widow at forty, with her family divided and the fate of her children uncertain.

David, one year older than Yvette, was also her first cousin.

Yvette and I nodded to Asher. *I hope we can make it*, I thought. *It is one thing for the two of us to take this dangerous and uncertain escape, but now we were eight people, including four young children.*

I am sure Yvette was thinking the same.

So here we were on Tuesday evening on our way to Yvette's parents' home to say goodbye and to pick up David, Tina, and her kids. Linda, the youngest of the kids, was waiting at the gate and ran into the house to announce our arrival. We paid the cab driver and walked in. Everyone was in the living room: Asher and Farha; Yvette's uncle Gurgi; his wife, Marcel, and son David; and Tina, surrounded by her children—Albert (age sixteen), Charly (thirteen), Edmond (eleven), and Linda (six). There was hardly any conversation, just lots of hugging, kissing, and tears.

Yvette's aunt Marcel, Gurgi's wife, handed me a half-liter bottle of scotch. "It is cold up north. This will warm you up."

"Okay, we have no time to waste. David, can you get us a cab? A large car or a van?" I asked. Then I turned to Tina and said, "I hope you don't have many suitcases."

She quickly pointed to a small brown suitcase and a duffel bag. I nodded. Tina looked like she was preparing for a lazy walk by the river. She wore a conservative white dress with a blue floral pattern, and her hair was covered by a light-blue scarf.

Yvette and I got in the front of the blue 1963 Impala. Tina, David, and the four kids scrambled in the back.

"Take us to the central train station," I said to the driver.

"Are we going on vacation?" the cab driver asked, trying to be friendly.

"Not really, just to visit family." I was abrupt and unfriendly, and the driver sensed it.

Silence fell on the car. We were on our way; there was no return. The kids in the back watched and heard everything. They understood what was going on and were unusually quiet and calm.

The day before, I had asked Saleh Is'hayek, Mom's cousin, to come over to our apartment. We told him of our plan to leave. He suggested that we give the key to the apartment to his Muslim partner, whom he trusted with his life.

"He will sell everything you have here and send you the money," Saleh said.

The Muslim partner came to take the key. "Don't worry," he assured us. "Go with God's help. Send me your address wherever you are, and I will send you the money." (He never sent us the money, and he ignored all of our correspondence.)

It was easier than I had thought it would be. In no time we were on the train platform among hundreds of people, passengers and those who came to see them off. As we climbed onto the train, I saw familiar faces. People from our community. We passed each other awkwardly, acting like strangers, each going to their own cabin. David shared our cabin, and Tina and her kids were in the adjoining cabin.

As the train moved out of the station, I felt relief. Maybe we would be safe for the next fourteen hours as the train chugged along on its way to Erbil. Thirty minutes into the trip, we heard a soft knock on our cabin door. I opened the door to see Elaine and her daughter, Vivian. Elaine's husband, a well-known attorney, refused to leave and stayed behind. A few months after we left, we heard that he had been taken by the Mukhabarat and disappeared.

"Did Naeem send you?" she asked as she closed the cabin door behind her.

"Yes," I said.

"Thank God we are going with someone we know."

In less than ten minutes, we had more visitors, three couples and five children: Albert P., his wife, and their five-year-old son; Yousuf A., his wife, their six-year-old son, and their four-year-old daughter; and Yousuf P., his wife, their three-year-old daughter, and a baby boy. We knew them all, and we had all been sent by Naeem to meet Saeed at the Erbil train station. For a few moments it felt like we were going to the north for a relaxing vacation. We spoke in low voices and in the Muslim dialect for fear of being overheard.

I had to kick everyone out of our cabin so we could get some sleep. However, I could not fall asleep that night. At the break of dawn, I sat by the cabin window to watch small, dimly lit villages and farms with lots of cows and sheep roll by. *How beautiful and peaceful everything looks from a distance,* I thought.

Around 6:00 a.m., the train slowed down and eventually stopped at Erbil station. Our dangerous adventure was about to begin.

CHAPTER 21

The Trip to the Border

W alking out of the station, the clamor of cab drivers was overwhelming, but not enough to distract us from the blinding bright sun, the cool fresh air, and the smell of freshly baked bread. I walked between the cab drivers calling, "Saeed! Are you Saeed? Saeed . . ." There was no Saeed to be found.

The area in front of the station was getting less and less crowded by the minute. The few people who were still there were checking out the vendors sitting on the ground with baskets full of fresh bread, cheeses, fruit, or vegetables. It seemed that no one was waiting for us, and we became more and more noticeable.

I could see two soldiers with machine guns by the station door watching us. We had to move. Albert P., his wife, and their son joined our group, so we were now eleven people. I asked a cab driver who was standing nearby, waiting for me to make up my mind, if he could take us to a good resort near Sulaymaniyah, a Kurdish town close to the Iranian border.

"Yes, sir, which resort?" he asked.

"I want the best one in the area," I said. "But we need two cars."

"No problem. Let's go." He grabbed the two duffel bags in one hand and Tina's small suitcase in the other and ran to a yellow-and-black Pontiac. As he put the bags in the trunk, he talked to another taxi driver standing next to a green-and-white Chevrolet Impala.

"Albert, you and your family take the Chevrolet, we will squeeze into the Pontiac," I said, then I ran back to buy some bread and cheese before catching up with the rest as they were getting in the cabs. As our car left the station, the driver became inquisitive. He looked at Linda in his rearview mirror, sitting on her mother's lap.

"Little one, where do you come from?"

Linda was quiet. She had been told not to talk to anyone.

"Baghdad," I said.

"Oh, you will love it here. It is cooler, and the air is fresher. Do any of you guys ski?"

"No, not really," I said.

"Oh, what a shame! We still have a lot of snow on the mountains, you will see. . . ."

No one answered; we were all busy eating the bread and cheese. The driver turned on the radio, blasting Kurdish songs.

I could see the kids in the back looking with curiosity at the people on the street in their traditional Kurdish costumes. The men wore *shoga*, the typical tight jacket, *sherwal*, a kind of fluffy pants twice the size of regular pants, and a *sorwin*, a thick fabric wrapped around their heads. The women wore long-sleeve vests or jackets with colorful, long overcoats over puffy pants. Their hats were velvet wrappings ornamented with beads or gold charms. None of the children had been this far from home before; this was a whole different world for them.

As we left town on a three-lane highway, I noticed there were no road signs. Thoughts started racing in my head. *Where is the cab driver taking us? I would not know the difference if he was heading back to Baghdad. Naeem had sent several families before us to Erbil, and we never heard back from any of them. Did they cross the border or were they being held somewhere?*

"Are we heading east?" I finally asked, careful not to show my ignorance.

"Yes, sir, we are heading northeast, toward the Iranian border," the driver said, looking at me. *That was too much information. Is he Saeed?* I wondered. *Or were all the drivers waiting at the station Saeed?*

"Is your name Saeed?" I asked.

"No, my name is Ferhad," he answered.

"Why are we going to the Iranian border?" I asked, like that was not what we wanted.

"Because . . . ," Ferhad answered slowly, "the best resorts in the area are along this road. You guys will love the place I am taking you to."

I looked at the back seat. Everyone was awake and quiet. *We got in this car willingly, and we left our fate in Ferhad's hands. . . . We have no control anymore.* I placed my hand on Yvette's, who was sitting next to me.

The driver looked in his mirror. "Two more cars are following us. Are they part of your group?" he asked.

Looking back, I saw our friends from last night following us. "Yes, we met them on the train last night, and they said they did not know which resort to go to. It seems they decided to follow us."

Suddenly, I was leading a group of twenty-one. *Do they know that they are being led by the blind?*

About an hour into our trip, the driver slowed down by several huts with roofs covered with dried palm tree fronds. "This is a great place. There is a small lake down there, and the food is authentic Kurdish," Ferhad announced.

"I would like to go a little farther from the city, if you don't mind," I said.

"The next resort is at least forty-five minutes from here," Ferhad said, "but I can take you there if you prefer."

"Yes, please, keep going. I will pay you." The four-car caravan drove on.

A similar conversation ensued as he stopped the car at two more resorts. My goal was to get as close to the border as possible.

At the fourth resort the driver stopped. "We passed Haj Omran [a town 120 miles from Erbil]. We are twenty minutes from the Iranian border," Ferhad said emphatically. "There are no more resorts. This is as far as I can go."

We got out of the car with our luggage, and the cold air hit us immediately. It was around noon. Our two cabs turned around and drove away. The two other cabs stopped to unload the rest of our friends. We started walking down a mild slope on a dirt path toward the huts, which sat along a winding creek with trees along its banks in the shadow of a snow-covered mountain.

"Are we at the right place?" Elaine asked as she dragged her daughter.

"I don't know," I said.

"What do you mean, you don't know?" Yousuf P. asked angrily. "We followed you all the way. Where are we?"

"I think we are close to the border, at least that's what the cab driver told us," I said impatiently.

"Take it easy," said Yousuf A. "Relax, we will see where it goes."

Funny, I thought, *three of the men on this journey are called Yousuf.*

When we found out that no one was waiting for us at the train station, my instinct told me to get out of the city fast and get as close to the Iranian border as possible. I knew I would feel safer among the Kurds and hoped that we would find our way across the border somehow.

That evening, Yvette, David, and I went down to the creek and sat by its bank. The night was chilly, the sound of rushing water was soothing, and the smell of greenery saturated the fresh air. As dusk was replaced by night, thousands of stars lit the sky, and the shadows of the trees covered the ground in the moonlight.

Yvette and David were reminiscing about their childhood adventures. They did not look like first cousins. Yvette, fair and skinny, had long black hair and dark brown eyes. David had tawny skin, light brown hair, and blue eyes. Now their hometown, Baghdad, was far behind them—it was nothing but a collection of memories.

I opened the bottle of scotch that David's mom had given me in Baghdad, and we each took a sip. We pointed out the different constellations shining brightly in the black sky. David took the scotch bottle and pulled out a pen from his shirt pocket.

"What are you doing?" I asked.

"To . . . memorialize . . . our departure . . . from hell . . . ," David said as he wrote on the bottle label. I still have that bottle. A few years ago, I took it out of the buffet and drank what was left in it. The taste of scotch took me back to that night. I could still hear the water rushing and feel the cold breeze on my face. I had goose bumps.

Mesmerized by the stars and a half-moon, the three of us became quiet and drifted into our own worlds. Racing thoughts overwhelmed me. *Have the authorities already found out that we left? Did they go into our apartment? Did they take our car? Will they go after my in-laws?* Questions, questions, questions . . .

And where do we go from here? I wondered. My parents were waiting for us in Holland, my brother was in the States,

The scotch bottle.

and my two sisters were in Israel, and none of them had the slightest idea that we were fleeing Iraq. *How will we contact them?* I became very anxious, and I suggested we go back to our cabin. We passed by Tina's cabin, where the kids were playing a game on the floor. Tina sat on the bed looking at them. She looked hopeful and turned to us and smiled. I was very happy they were with us.

I wanted to be alone to think, so instead of going back to our cabin with Yvette and David, I climbed up to the main road. The road, lit by the moon and the stars, was deserted and quiet. I took a few steps and stopped. I was not alone. I heard the sound of footsteps on the dirt. *Crunch, crunch, crunch.* Suddenly, a man in Kurdish attire came out of the dark. His oversized jacket and baggy trousers made him look twice his size. Bushy gray eyebrows below the red-and-white turban dominated his face. My heartbeat quickened.

"*Massa' al-Kher* [Good evening]," the man greeted me. "Do you want to go across the border?"

His direct question shocked me. I wanted to say yes but couldn't. What if he was a government agent? On the other hand, he might be the one we were looking for. *This is not the time to chicken out*, I thought.

"Yes," I said.

"How many people do you have with you?"

"We are twenty-one altogether," I said with a contorted face.

He stared at me for a long time. *Maybe we are too many?*

"Alright. Bring everyone here at eleven o'clock tonight," he finally said and turned around and disappeared into the darkness. I did not even have a chance to utter a word.

I shook my head in disbelief. I didn't even get a good look at the man's face, but I was sure he didn't look like a smuggler. *What does a smuggler look like anyway?* I wondered. *Well,* I told myself, *it is too late now.*

CHAPTER 22

Journey Through the Night

"I found someone who will take us across the border tonight," I announced after the whole group gathered in our cabin. I was expecting happy and excited responses. It turned out that I was wrong.

"Did Naeem send him?" asked Elaine.

"I don't know."

"What is his name?" asked the calm Yousuf A.

"I don't know."

"You trust a man that came out of nowhere? What if he is a government agent?" asked the anxious Yousuf P. with the baby in his arms.

"I don't know."

"We are doomed. They will take us back to Baghdad!" said Elaine with tears running down her cheeks.

"Did he want money?" asked Yousuf A.

"No."

"Then he is definitely an agent. Maybe we should leave before he comes back with the police." Albert P. spoke for the first time.

"How can we leave? There is no one to take us back tonight," Yousuf P. said. He was so angry his face was all red.

Finally, I spoke up. "My family and I will wait for this man at the main road at eleven tonight. Anyone who wants to come with us is welcome."

"You are crazy. Do you know if this man will even show up?" Yousuf A. asked.

"He will," I responded confidently.

"How do you know he will take us across the border? What if he delivers us to the Iraqi police?"

"Stop, stop, everyone," I said as I stood up. "You do not have to come with us."

Everyone walked out of our cabin grumbling.

"Are you sure it is safe to go with this guy?" Yvette asked.

"No, I am not sure. Maybe I should have checked his references," I said with a smile. "But seriously, do we know who to trust? Can we trust the next person we find?"

Just before eleven, we left our cabin and walked up to the main road. I held Charly's and Edmond's hands. Yvette, with Linda clinging to her and the duffel bag in her hand, followed. She was dressed in a white shirt and a knee-length dark-blue skirt. Her long black hair was covered with a blue scarf. David, Tina, and Albert followed us.

Elaine and her daughter, Vivian, ran up the hill to catch up with us. Elaine wore a black pair of pants. *What is she thinking?* I thought to myself. *Doesn't she know that that could be disrespectful to the locals?*

The three couples and their five children were already on

the main road, waiting for us with their small bags. Yousuf P., short and stocky, was still in his gray suit. He stood next to his wife, who carried their baby, while his daughter clinged to him, as the mild breeze played with the few hairs on his head. The calm Yousuf A., tall, his skin naturally tanned, and his hair oiled and well combed, wore a white shirt and black pants and held his wife's hand, and Albert P., who was a few years older than me, wore a T-shirt and jeans and had his arm wrapped around his wife's shoulders. The three younger children were playing with the pebbles on the pavement. Looks were exchanged without words. We were all very nervous. We gazed into the darkness enveloping us.

Suddenly, bright headlights pierced the darkness in the distance. They drew closer and closer. A large black pickup with a canvas camper shell over its bed stopped in front of us. I raised my hand above my eyes to block the bright light.

The Kurd with whom I spoke earlier got out of the truck. A dark mole was very prominent on his right cheek. *I must have been too scared to notice that before*, I thought. He gestured to us to follow him as he walked to the back of the truck. He lifted the canvas curtains, revealing two benches facing each other.

"*Is'adoo* [Climb in]!" he ordered.

The truck bed had two steps but no tailgate. Everyone climbed into the back of the truck and sat on the benches quietly. Yvette, holding Linda's hand, looked at me. The two benches were fully occupied, and the three of us were still outside the truck. I climbed up and sat on the edge of the bench to my right, pushing everyone in. Yvette and Linda then climbed up. Yvette sat on my lap and Linda on hers.

The Kurd dropped down the curtain and tied it tightly to the floor of the truck bed. We were in complete darkness; we could hear each other's breathing, but we could not see each other's faces.

The process went so smoothly and quickly, as if it had been pre-rehearsed. Before the Kurd slammed the passenger door closed, the truck jolted forward and accelerated. The sudden and abrupt movement of the truck caused everyone to slide on the benches toward the back. There was nothing for me to hold on to. Part of me was already off the bench; my left leg pushed against the canvas curtain, and my left foot dangled out of the truck. A cold breeze blew through the curtain. The person sitting next to us grabbed my right arm and pulled the three of us back onto the bench.

We sat in the dark and swayed from side to side as the truck zigzagged on a curvy mountain road at great speed. I held Yvette and Linda tightly so they would not fall out of the truck. The Kurd and the driver conversed calmly in Kurdish, their cigarette smoke permeating the truck.

Twenty minutes later the truck stopped.

"Are we there?" someone whispered.

The curtain was untied and lifted over the top of the truck. The taillights of the truck painted the narrow mountain road red. This time the Kurd spoke slowly and in a very low voice.

"Run and hide in the forest," he said, pointing to the left of the road. "Someone will come to pick you up in ten minutes."

We got off the truck and walked off the road in one line. The ground sloped down and was lightly covered with brush. The tall, dense trees may have been only two hundred feet away from the road, but at that moment they seemed to be two thousand feet away.

"Run . . . run . . . don't make noise. Hide between the trees," the Kurd repeated in a low, calm voice.

We hurried through the brush and into the trees. We heard the truck turn around, and all we could see were the red taillights speeding away in the distance. Surrounded by the tall trees and their shadows, we looked at each other. Behind us, the narrow road hugging the mountain stood stark against a background of thousands of stars.

The deafening silence was interrupted by the occasional howling of wolves in the distance. The children were quiet and scared and held on to their parents. With the sleeping baby in his arms, the anxious Yousuf P. crouched down and sat on the ground with his legs to one side. One by one we all sat down.

Suddenly, Yousuf P.'s baby woke up, looked around, and started crying. His shrieks echoed in the quiet night. Everyone panicked.

"Keep him quiet," someone shushed.

Yousuf P. covered the baby's mouth with his hand. The baby, unable to breath, started coughing. His coughs echoed back twice. Soon, the wolves joined in, and the silence was shattered. My heart stopped. Luckily, in a couple of moments, the baby stopped crying.

Here we were, twenty-one people hiding on the side of a mountain, in the shadows of trees. I do not know what was going on in everyone's head; I was numb and felt like a spectator waiting for the next scene to unfold. It may have been an hour later, but it felt like an eternity, when we saw headlights coming from the east. The truck slowed down and turned left, blocking the road, shining its headlights on the forest behind us before stopping.

We were exposed; there was no place to hide.

"*Ta'alou, ta'alou bil ajal* [Come, come quickly]," a hurried call came from the road as the silhouette of a man appeared in front of the headlights.

Without thinking, everyone got up and started to run toward the truck. I ran behind Albert, carrying Linda and dragging Edmond with my right hand. Charly held on to my jacket as he ran next to me.

One by one, the group climbed into the back of the truck. No instructions this time. Yvette sat at the end of the bench and pushed people in to make space for me. Linda sat on my lap. The curtain came down between us and the world, and the truck backed off the gravel shoulder onto the road, accelerating east.

After ten long minutes of speeding on a curvy road, the truck stopped. The driver talked to men on the road. We heard laughter and money changing hands. The truck then moved, this time at a slower speed.

"Anyone in the back want a cigarette?" the question came from the front of the truck. "We just bought a few cartons from a smuggler." Laughter followed. Some of us would have killed for a cigarette, but no one dared to speak.

Minutes later, the truck stopped again. This time the conversation was in Farsi and sounded serious. There was a lighter's flick, followed by the smell of smoke from freshly lit cigarettes. Then came the sound of a boom gate going up. The truck drove slowly down a bumpy road, with the streetlights seeping through the gaps at the curtain's edges.

Chapter 23

Freedom at Last

The truck stopped, and this time the engine was turned off. The curtain was lifted.

"*Ahlan wa sahlan, tafadhaloo* [Welcome, come in, please]." A blondish man in Western clothing welcomed us. It was clear that Arabic was not his native tongue.

Two young men helped everyone off the truck under the watchful eyes of the blondish man. We were directed to a large tent on the side of the road. Inside, the tent was brightly lit. We were seated in a circle and offered hot tea in big Persian-style glasses.

"Welcome to Iran. Welcome to freedom," said the blondish man, who stood in the middle of the circle. "My name is Zev," he continued. We looked at each other. "Yes, I am Jewish," he affirmed with a smile after noticing the surprise on our faces. "I would like you to tell me your name and whether you have family in Israel." He turned around, making eye contact with everyone. "Who wants to go first?"

Everyone was quiet.

"We would like to inform your families and relatives that you are out of Iraq."

We looked at each other, wondering what we should do. Should we admit that we have family in Israel?

"My name is Yousuf Dabby, and I have two sisters in Israel," I blurted out.

"What are their names?" Zev was writing on a yellow pad.

"Albertine Gibly and Tikva Natanel," I answered slowly.

"What cities do they live in?" he asked.

"Tel Barukh," I said.

"Is this lady with you?" he asked, looking at Yvette.

"Yes," I answered. "My wife, Yvette Atraghji. Her stepsister Rachel Drori lives in Tel Aviv."

Zev wrote down the names, drew a line across the yellow pad, and looked at Tina, who was sitting next to Yvette. "And you, miss, what is your name?"

He went around the circle till he had everyone's information written on his pad.

"We will take you now to a hotel where you will spend the night, and tomorrow you will travel to Tehran," he announced.

I stood up and looked around the tent. My fellow passengers sat in a circle, sipping hot tea. It felt unreal. Like a prisoner just released, anxiety and uncertainty overshadowed freedom. I was numb and exhausted.

We left the tent and walked about a block to a two-story yellow brick building. In the vestibule, we passed two older men in their underwear playing backgammon.

"*Doo shesh* [Double sixes]!" called the man rolling the dice as he slammed the checkers on the backgammon board. The two men were too engrossed in the game and did not even bother to look up as we passed them. *Life goes on,* Mom used to say, *kul wehid mit'azee be'ezanoo* (everyone is occupied by their problem). Their backgammon game was more important to them than a bunch of refugees who had just made it to freedom.

Our room was very small, the walls were bare, and yellow ceramic tiles covered the floor. One full-size bed and a two-drawer cabinet made up the furniture. The oversized window overlooked the main street of the small village—Khaneh, we later learned.

We fell into bed, exhausted, in the early hours of the morning. Lying on the bed, Yvette and I watched the lizards crawl across the white ceiling. I had always wondered why these beige lizards didn't fall off the smooth ceiling. *Now our lives were upside down. And just like the lizards, we will adapt to it too,* I thought. *But where do we go from here?* I wondered.

Before our wedding, Yvette's father asked me where we planned to live after leaving Iraq. "Israel," I answered with certainty, but I did not tell him about my dream to enlist in the Israeli army. Persecution had reinforced my Jewishness, and torture and imprisonment only strengthened my desire to fight back. Our first stop, though, would have to be Holland, where my parents were waiting.

I must have dozed off, only to be abruptly awakened by shouting on the street. I looked at my watch. It was 6:00 a.m. I rushed to the window. Young men in khakis were directing a bus to park by the hotel door. They spoke on walkie-talkies.

"Do I hear Hebrew?" Yvette asked as she was getting up.

"Yes, and a bus is already here," I answered.

We went downstairs and were told to get on the bus. When everyone in our group was on the bus, our fourteen-hour journey to Tehran started. This was our first day out of Iraq, Friday, July 30, 1971.

The bus pulled into Tehran around 9:00 p.m. The city was alive. The streets were brightly lit and busy. Stores were open, and restaurants were crowded.

"Why are the streets decorated?" Yvette asked the driver in English. We were sitting at the front of the bus, just behind the driver.

"Next month we will celebrate the 2,500-year anniversary of the Persian Empire," the driver answered with pride. "The festivities and celebrations planned will be unlike any other anywhere in the world."

Two and a half millennia, that's how long we lived in the land known as Iraq, I thought. It broke my heart that yesterday we had left our motherland to become stateless refugees.

In Tehran the bus took us to the Commodore Hotel. As we got off the bus, it dawned on me that we were no longer scared—we were free. I could not help but see the big smile on Tina's face as she stood there surrounded by her four children—Albert, Charly, Edmond, and Linda.

As the widow of a martyr whose life was taken because he was Jewish, Tina and her children were welcomed by Israel. Albert went on to become an Israeli diplomat. Sadly, on August 20, 1985, he was assassinated in Cairo. He was thirty.

The hotel room that night may have looked more luxurious than it really was after the primitive inn at Khaneh. We learned that our families in Israel had been notified the moment we were identified in the tent after we crossed the border. Early the next morning, my brother, Charles (Saleh changed his name to Charles when he got to Israel), called from Los Angeles. It was the first time we had heard each other's voices. He was as excited as we were.

"What are your plans?" Charles asked.

"Can't wait to go to Israel."

"No, Yousuf, you have to come to the States first," Charles said.

"But Charles, I have been dreaming of going to Israel." I was determined. "But first, I want to see Mom and Dad in Holland."

"Okay, go to Holland for now, join our parents," Charles said after a long pause. "I will come too. We can talk there."

That morning I was taken to the Israeli embassy in Tehran. I met with three men who seemed to know as much, if not more, than me about the Jewish community in Baghdad. We sat around a long conference table in a room in the basement of the building.

"You must go back to Baghdad," the oldest of the three said.

I thought he was joking, but he looked very serious.

"No one knows that you left the country yet," the man with the black curly hair added. He was the youngest of the three. "You can go back and help others to escape."

For a moment I thought, *Maybe I should go back. But this time, if they catch me, they will for sure hang me.*

"You should know that we have been working hard to get the Jewish community out of Iraq," said the man who looked European, with his fair skin, blond hair, and blue eyes. "Do you think that you are here because you were lucky? Do you think that the people who drove you to Haj Omran and those who took you across the border were doing it out of the goodness of their hearts?"

Left to right: Edmond, Charly, me, Yvette, and Albert,
Tehran, December, 1970.

Oh my God. These people planned everything. After all,
all the cab drivers were Saeed. Naeem was the messenger; in
the meantime, he was enriching himself. These people helped
us get out, and now they are asking me to work with them and
help others get out. Here I was, about to start a new life, have a
family, and live in freedom. Do I really want to go back into the
lion's den? What are the chances that I can get out again? And
what about Yvette? What will she do? Wait here, maybe I will
come back? On the other hand, if I go back, I could help many
desperate people get out. But am I capable of being that kind of
fearless operative? I don't believe so.

"I cannot go back," I said. "I will be caught, and I may en-
danger the people I contact."

The older man leaned forward. "I can understand that."

"You can still help us reach out to your friends," the European man said. "Could you write small messages to them?" He sat back in his chair. "Write something that's privy to you and them, so they can trust our messenger."

"I can do that," I said. The three men watched as I sketched the directions to a few of my friends' homes. I wrote a note to each on small pieces of paper about incidents or conversations that only the two of us shared. I left the Israeli embassy feeling good. *My friends will be really surprised,* I thought.

The decision not to go back to Baghdad weighed heavily on me for several days. To this day, I keep telling myself that I did the right thing, that there is no way I could have succeeded in such a mission while living in fear of being discovered. I just was not brave enough.

We stayed in Tehran for thirteen busy days. Our time in Iran opened our eyes to the importance of Israel as a Jewish homeland that looks after the Jews everywhere. Israel may have been the reason that Arabs hate us, but Israel was also the reason we stayed alive. Iran issued us *parwanat eboor* (laissez-passers), which allowed us to stay in the country for fifteen days. Over the next few months, this document would serve as a travel document for us, since we were stateless.

At the time, there were around 100,000 Jews in Iran, and approximately 1,500 of them were of Iraqi origin. The Jews were not discriminated against and were treated well during the Shah's reign. However, they all knew that everything could change radically if the Shah was gone.

Parwanat eboor (Iranian laissez-passer), 1971.

Ad in an Iraqi newspaper on October 7, 1971, listing names of Jews who escaped the country and ordering them to report to the naturalization office within seven days to avoid losing their nationality:
No. 12: Yousuf I. and his wife and two children.
No. 28: Yousuf P. and his wife and two children.
No. 29: Yousuf Haskel Yousuf Dabby and his wife,
Yvette Asher Ezra Atarghji.

CHAPTER 24

The Story of Saleh

O ur life and future were determined in the first two weeks we spent in Holland.

On Wednesday, August 12, 1971, we flew out of Tehran to Amsterdam. The Dutch consulate in Tehran issued us visas to enter Holland, and the Hebrew Immigrant Aid Society (HIAS) paid for our airfares. As we walked out of the terminal in Amsterdam, I saw my parents. Tears ran down my cheeks as we ran toward each other. We were lost for words; we just hugged and hugged. They came with Rosy (Yvette's sister), her husband, Albert, and Ezra (Yvette's brother) to meet us at the airport.

Holland welcomed Jews arriving from Iraq as refugees under the umbrella of the United Nations High Commissioner for Refugees and offered to integrate them as Dutch citizens.

The Joods Maatschapplijk Werk ("Jewish social services"), or JMW, attended to the Jewish refugees' needs. It provided them temporary lodging at the Hotel Stadhouderskade in Amsterdam (Hotel Blossoms, currently) and made sure that the refugees

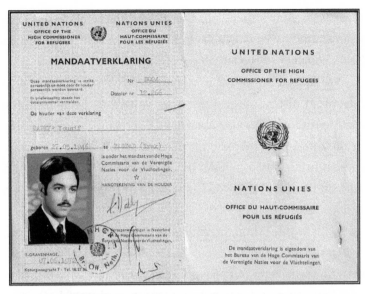

Our refugee IDs, 1971, issued by the Office of the United Nations High Commissioner for Refugees (UNHCR).

received weekly stipends to cover their financial needs. Those who wanted to learn Dutch could do so at a boarding school in Zeist, courtesy of the Dutch government.

We joined around thirty Iraqi refugees for dinner in the basement of the hotel. Everyone wanted to hear about our escape and about their family still in Baghdad. They were excited and they talked over each other. The hotel manager came down to the basement to visit with us. He looked around and said to me, "Everyone is talking at the same time. Who is listening?"

He is right, I thought, *everyone wants to tell their story.*

In the morning Ezra took us to get our refugee papers and get into the system. A black man who wore earrings helped us.

"Is it common for men here to wear earrings?" I asked.

"Some men do. But can't you tell that this guy is gay?" Ezra asked. "Gay people are free to be themselves here," he added when he saw my surprise. I had never interacted with a gay man who was not afraid of showing his femininity. I was sure the man who helped us could sense my awkwardness. I felt bad. *More than anyone, I should understand that we are all the same, regardless of our sexual orientation.*

A few days later, my brother flew in from the States. Charles was five-foot-four and had many of Dad's features—his nose shape, hazel eyes, and thinning hair. We were all overcome with emotions and cried when we met him in the hotel lobby.

I met Charles for the first time when I was in London for my surgery in 1961 and he was in London for work. Mom and I visited him at his hotel and spent around an hour with him. I found him more serious this time, and I got to know him better.

Saleh (Charles), 1974.

That evening, we sat down in our hotel room and talked. Charles recounted how he was smuggled out of Basra to Abadan in Iran. Uncle Khadouri put him on a rowboat with two fishermen, who covered him with netting and rowed across the Shatt al-Arab River to Iran. Charles then traveled to Istanbul, where Dad wanted him to finish high school. But Charles had other plans and flew to Israel instead.

"I was planning to stay a few weeks at Aunt Salima's till I found a job and a place to live," Charles told us. Aunt Salima was Mom's younger sister; she and her family had moved to Tel Aviv in the early 1940s, eight years before the state of Israel was born.

"I got to Aunt Salima's house in the early afternoon. She was shocked to see me at her door. She told me that her house was full, and she could not take me in." Charles' eyes teared up as he continued. "'But Aunt,' I pleaded with her, 'I have no place to go.' She told me, 'Find a kibbutz.' She didn't even invite me in. I walked away confused and scared."

My parents and I sat spellbound listening to Charles.

"Then I remembered Aunt Gurgiyi," Charles continued, "so I took the bus to Jerusalem." Aunt Gurgiyi was the wife of Elia, Dad's brother. She took care of Dad and his brother Khadouri when they ran away from home. Elia passed away young, and Aunt Gurgiyi moved in with her sister Chahla Bibi, who emigrated to Israel in the early 1940s.

"When Aunt Gurgiyi opened the door, she exclaimed with joy, 'Saleh, I have been waiting for you!' She hugged me and told me that Dad appeared in her dream the night before and asked her to take care of me."

Dad was very emotional and choked back tears, so I ran to bring him a glass of water.

"The Bibis' apartment was very crowded, but Mr. Bibi welcomed me, and using a curtain, he made a private space for me in a small room where two of his kids slept."

Charles went on to tell us that Mr. Bibi treated him like a son and gave him a job as a mechanic in a body shop owned by his nephew Benyamin. "One day Mr. Bibi saw me crying, and when I told him I didn't like the job of a mechanic because it was dirty, he put his hands on my shoulder and told me not to worry, I could work in his store, where he sold dried fruits and nuts."

My parents were speechless and cried. Charles told us that he stayed with the Bibis for a couple of months and moved to

Tel Aviv when he received funds from Dad. He used the funds to purchase a small apartment near Shkhunat HaTikva, a poor section of Tel Aviv.

"And how did Berta and Tikva find you?" Mom asked.

"A social worker brought them to my apartment," Charles replied. "The girls, like all immigrants from Arab lands, were sprayed with DDT as they left the plane. The aunts and their families were taken to the *ma'abara* [transition tent camp], where they lived for almost two years before they were moved to government housing."

"My sisters sent messages saying do not come," Mom said. "They had a rough time. I cannot even imagine their transition from a leisurely life in Baghdad to tents and rationed essentials."

There was silence for a few moments, each of us drifting in our own thoughts.

"Although I was happy to be reunited with my sisters, I was also scared," Charles went on to say. "Suddenly at seventeen I found myself responsible for two more people."

"Oh my God, oh my God," Mom moved back and forth in her chair. "What did we do to our children?"

"We felt abandoned, with no one to advise us," Charles continued. "Berta and I did not finish high school. Berta worked in the post office, and I worked as a tourist guide. Tikva finished high school and took courses in accounting."

"Your aunts could not help you?" Mom asked.

"Our aunts had their own problems," Charles retorted. "We visited them every week and cried with them. Life was difficult for everyone. Israel was overwhelmed with immigrants, and food and other essentials were hard to find."

Mom wiped her tears. These were very tough stories for my parents to hear.

"Do you remember when we wrote to you about the flooding of our area and the extensive damage to the apartment?" Charles asked. Dad nodded, and Charles went on. "We were so grateful that you sent us money. I purchased an apartment in the center of Ramat Gan and furnished it nicely. Imagine, in those days we had a refrigerator and a washer in the apartment. We were very comfortable."

"Did you serve in the army?" Dad asked.

"For sure. I was in intelligence, and I was in Lebanon for a long time."

"My God," Mom said. "You were in Lebanon? Were you a spy?"

"Sort of." Charles smiled. "I escaped just in time when my cover was blown. My boss told me that my next mission would be in Baghdad."

Mom gasped.

"But I told my boss I couldn't go to Baghdad because my parents and little brother were still there. He didn't care. 'Don't look them up, pretend they are not there,' he told me." Charles became very emotional. "What was he thinking? How could I stop myself from seeing you if I was so close to you?"

"Did you come to Baghdad?" Dad asked anxiously.

"No, I am not that crazy," Charles said. "I pretended I was sick and resigned from the mission." Charles leaned back in his seat. "My boss knew I was lying, but he let me off that mission; we are still good friends." Charles smiled.

Charles's story continued during and after dinner. He spoke about my sisters' marriages. "When Aharon proposed to Berta in 1955, we wrote to you asking for your permission," Charles told Dad. "And you immediately sent your approval."

"I actually knew Aharon very well because he had worked at my bank in Baghdad," Dad said. "He was gentle and smart, and I liked him."

"You also approved of Tikva's marriage to Edmond in 1962," Charles said.

"Of course, you told me he was a smart accountant and a good person," Dad said.

"It was very difficult for us not to be with our daughters on their wedding days," Mom said. "It was even more difficult when they had children and I was not with them."

"You will love your six grandchildren when you see them in Israel," Charles said. "I talked to my sisters on the phone before I left Los Angeles, and they can't wait to see you."

"And what did you do after your military service?" Mom asked.

"I continued to work as a tourist guide." Charles sat up and became very animated. "Then the best thing happened to me. One day I took a lovely older Italian couple on a tour of northern Israel. They loved me, gave me a big tip, and asked me to drive them to the airport the next day. Before I left them at the airport, I gave them a small Bible as a gift. They hugged me and said goodbye. As they walked away, the man suddenly turned to me and asked, 'Do you want to work for me in Rome?' Without hesitating, I said, 'Sure, I would love to.'"

Charles took a sip of water and went on to tell us that it turned out that the man owned a large tourism company associated with Fiat. Charles went to Rome in the early 1960s and worked for the Italian company for a couple of years before becoming the company's representative in the United States.

"I opened an office for the company in New York and another one in Chicago," Charles said. "When I arrived in Los Angeles in 1968, I fell in love with the city. It reminded me of Baghdad: wide streets, palm trees, and moderate weather year-round. I decided to stay in California." Charles started his own travel agency and got married in Los Angeles.

Charles wanted us to join him in Los Angeles. However, we were still planning to settle in Israel, where we could build a home among our family and friends.

"Come to the States," Charles pleaded. "Get your American papers first; you can always go to Israel."

"But then our life will be on hold," I said. "How long will we have to wait for the green cards?"

"Six months, maybe even less," Charles assured us. "I have reached out to a congressman who assured me that he would help you."

Eventually, Charles talked Yvette and me into waiting for our American papers in Holland. On September 7, 1971, we drove my parents to Brussels, where they took a flight to Israel to finally join their two daughters.

CHAPTER 25

Holland

Holland, at that time, was inundated by young Americans who were trying to avoid serving in Vietnam. They set up tents in parks and spent their days and nights smoking marijuana, which was legal in Holland. I could not fully understand at the time why these young men fled their country rather than fight for the freedom of others. They took freedom for granted.

"Don't they realize that if they don't fight for freedom everywhere, the day may come when they will lose theirs?" I told Yvette. "We had to flee our country for freedom!" *The first thing I will do when I get to the U.S.*, I thought, *is to get drafted in the army and fight for the freedom of others.* Soon after arriving in Los Angeles, I went to an army recruitment office to register. The soldier in charge looked at my new green card.

"Go home to your family, son," he said. "In two weeks you will turn twenty-seven, and you will not be subject to the draft."

I was confused at the time, but in hindsight I was lucky.

The Portuguese Synagogue in Amsterdam.

While we waited for our green cards, Yvette and I learned the Dutch language at a boarding school in Zeist, a beautiful little town thirty-five miles southeast of Amsterdam, well known for its gardens and quaint cottages.

On Yom Kippur in 1971, we attended Kol Nidre services in the Esnoga, the Spanish Portuguese synagogue. The magnificent Esnoga was constructed in 1675 by the Sephardic community of Amsterdam, most of whom had escaped from Spain and Portugal to flee the Inquisition. Services were held in the light of hundreds of candles, placed in beautiful chandeliers and on candleholders, because the building had no electricity. The prayers in Dutch and Ladino, both foreign to us, were magical.

On November 29, 1971, we were very excited to welcome Yvette's parents to Amsterdam. Finally, both of our families were out of Iraq. We were relieved. Rachel (Yvette's sister) came

Left to right: Rachel, Ron, Asher, Farha, Yvette,
Naima, Haskel, and Ovadia (Rachel's husband).

from Florida with her ten-year-old son to see her parents. After a couple of weeks, Rachel and her son flew with her parents to Israel to help them settle.

On more than one occasion, I was asked by the JMW to go to Amsterdam Airport to verify and welcome new Jewish refugees arriving from Iraq. Helping others was a very gratifying experience.

To process our applications for emigration to the States, the American consulate had asked for our birth and marriage certificates, which we did not have with us. Before leaving Iraq, Yvette's mother managed to get our marriage certificate and my birth certificate from the Jewish Community Office in Baghdad and brought them with her to Amsterdam. In lieu of Yvette's birth certificate, Albert's mother and Morris Shabi, another older refugee, had to appear before the American consul in Amsterdam to confirm the date of Yvette's birth.

I did not like being dependent on the Jewish Organization, and I wanted to do something productive rather than just walk around Amsterdam every day, so I searched for a job. I found an opening for a civil engineer in a prefab concrete factory in Utrecht, and although I thought my chances of getting the job were slim, I applied. To my surprise, following my interview, I was offered the job. I was ecstatic.

Utrecht is about thirty miles east of Amsterdam. To travel to my new job every day, I took the tram to the central train station in Amsterdam, where I got on the train to Utrecht and then took the bus to the factory, a one-hour trip. To stay warm in the cold and windy winter of Amsterdam, I wore a long woolen coat on top of layers of sweaters and thermal pants, a wool scarf around my neck, warm gloves, and long warm boots. Icicles formed on my mustache while walking the short distance from the hotel to the tram station along the frozen canal.

At work I did better than I had thought I would at communicating with other workers and at writing reports in Dutch. The work system in Holland was nothing like the system I later came to know in the United States. We had two coffee breaks, one at midmorning and one in midafternoon, and a long lunch break. The atmosphere was very relaxed, and deadlines were flexible. When I submitted my first report to my boss on the same day he requested it, he was shocked.

"This report takes three days to prepare," he told me. "Take it back, relax the rest of the day, and bring it to me tomorrow."

The job was not exactly my dream job, but I felt good to be able to adapt to the Dutch system so fast.

Two months into the job, in March 1972, we heard from the American consulate: Our U.S. papers were ready, and we were to have an interview with the consul.

"You are both civil engineers?" the consul asked us.

Yvette and I nodded and smiled.

"I am sad for you," she said. "Engineers are a dime a dozen in the States."

We felt uneasy, but the lady's remark did not dampen our excitement. The green cards came in a sealed envelope to be opened by the immigration officers at any U.S. airport.

Yvette and I decided to visit Israel before going to the States. Charles was very nervous that we might decide to stay in Israel. He booked our flights to Los Angeles from London at the end of April and planned to meet us in Israel. We applied for visas to visit Israel and England. The visa to England took almost one month to secure.

Holland will always hold a special place in my heart. It is a very crowded country that pays its citizens to emigrate to other countries, yet its doors are open to refugees from all over the world. Holland helped our parents and other Iraqi Jews to leave Iraq by issuing them entry visas and offered us citizenship and a new home where we could build a new life. Many Iraqi refugees took that offer and made Holland their new home, including Yvette's sister and brother-in-law, Rosy and Albert; her brother, Ezra; and mother's brother, Ezra, who left Iraq a few years later.

Holland is where Yvette and I finally started our lives in freedom, and where we planned our future.

CHAPTER 26

The Family Reunion

We flew to Israel from Amsterdam via Geneva. Before boarding the plane to Israel, we were searched thoroughly. The El Al personnel were very suspicious of us because we had an Iranian laissez-passer and we were born in Iraq. A man sitting behind us on the plane watched us the whole time; he even followed me when I went to the restroom. I am sure he noticed our excitement as the plane flew over Israel.

Stepping on Israeli soil was exhilarating. It was a moment we never thought would happen. My sisters and parents met us at the airport. We stayed with my parents in their apartment in Ramat Gan. Charles arrived in Tel Aviv a few days after we did.

"I came all the way to make sure you are coming with me to the States. I miss having family in Los Angeles," he told us, more than once.

On our first day together, my parents, Charles, Yvette, and I went to visit with my sisters at Tikva's home in Tel Barukh, a suburb of Tel Aviv. I had been looking forward to sitting down

Family reunion, 1972. Back row: Me, Berta, Tikva, and Charles. Front row: Naima and Haskel.

with my sisters and getting to know them. Berta, Tikva, and their husbands, Aharon and Edmond, were all there. We hugged and kissed.

Finally, our whole family was in one room.

Berta has Mom's features—black curly hair, dark brown eyes, lightly tanned skin, very energetic, and speaks fast. Tikva has Dad's big eyes and Mom's tanned skin. Charles has Dad's thin hair, large forehead, hazel green eyes, and his nose.

Everyone had a big smile on their faces. They talked about Israel, its weather, and its people, and, naturally, Mom and Dad wanted to know about their old friends.

I looked at my sisters and saw them as teenagers getting off the plane and being sprayed with DDT. I saw them clinging to their aunt's arms as a social worker was trying to separate them. Their parents were not there to protect them; they must have felt abandoned. I cannot even imagine what was going in their minds and how they managed.

At the time, my parents believed that sending the two girls to Israel ahead of them was the right thing to do. When they could not leave to join their daughters, that decision became disastrous. Both my sisters' and parents' suffering is inconceivable, and our parents must have regretted their decision a million times.

Their decision affected me also. What would my life have been like had I grown up with my siblings and was showered with their love?

Suddenly silence fell on the room.

"We had everything we wanted, but we had no parents to protect and guide us," Berta said.

"We were rich orphans," Tikva said.

Mom bit her lips and tears ran down her cheeks. Dad's face turned red.

The girls told us their story. How they were separated from their aunt and taken to Charles, who did his best, but he was also young and inexperienced. They recounted how every week they would take the bus to visit their aunt, who lived in a tent in the *ma'abara* (transition camp), where they all sat and cried.

Berta told us how she delivered the gold items Dad sent to a friend of his. When Dad arrived in Israel, his friend asked him for the items; fortunately, Berta had kept the receipt he signed when he took them from her. We sat and listened with awe at what they went through.

What happened in our family is not unique. Several families were divided by similar decisions. Times were difficult, and many families faced the same predicament and made the same choices.

At every social event we went to, someone approached us and introduced themselves as a cousin or a close relative. We never thought we had such large families. I was very excited to see Uncle Khadouri, Aunt Simha, and my cousins, and I spent a lot of time with them. We met my uncles Daoud and Salman and their families, and Charles also made sure that we met the Bibi family and Gurgiyi, who had taken care of my dad and Khadouri when they were young and also took care of Charles when he arrived in Israel. We also spent time with Yvette's parents and visited with her extended familiy and relatives.

Charles wanted us to see all of Israel. He drove us all over, from Rosh Hanikra in the north to Eilat in the south. He drove us across the Sinai (which was under Israeli control at the time) to visit Saint Catherine's Monastery at the base of Mount Sinai (Mount Horeb), where Moses received the Ten Commandments. The monastery is one of the oldest, still-working Christian monasteries in the world. It was built between 548 and 556 CE at the place where God appeared to Moses (the burning bush).

We stayed at a kibbutz in the north where my aunt Regina (one of Mom's sisters) and her husband, Saleem, the kibbutz baker, lived. Regina and Saleem were simple and good-natured people compared to the family in the city. They spent all their lives in the kibbutz, where every resident had a job and worked for the benefit of the community. Aunt Regina and her husband seemed happy and satisfied with what they had. They were excited that in two years they would be able to make a trip to Europe. *Would*

I be happy to live like that? No, I don't think so, I thought. I was eager to jump at life, to fulfil my dreams, motivated to move up in the world, hoping to make a difference. *Am I being selfish?*

The month we stayed in Israel was memorable to say the least. It did not feel like the country was at war. Israel was much better and safer than we had been led to believe. Young children walked to school alone with their house keys hanging around their necks. No one worried that a terrorist might be waiting around the corner. The population was very diverse and so was the food. It felt like being in Europe with a touch of the Middle East. Tel Aviv was a crowded city that never slept. The freedom and lack of fear were both new to us.

On the twenty-fourth anniversary of Israel's Independence Day, April 18, 1972, we joined thousands of Israelis in the center of Tel Aviv to celebrate. Singing and dancing with other Jews freely and proudly was an amazing experience, something we never in our wildest dreams thought we would do one day. The pride and patriotism people around us felt were contagious.

Throughout our stay in Israel, we felt uncertain about our decision to start our lives in the States. "Are we doing the right thing?" I asked Yvette. "Our parents and siblings are here, and our friends are happy here. Maybe we should stay here."

"You can't do that to Charles," Yvette replied. "He came all the way to make sure we don't change our minds. The least we can do is to check it out."

CHAPTER 27

Los Angeles

We arrived in London on Thursday, April 26, 1972.
The British officers at the airport did not want to let us in.

"You have visitors' visas," the officer at the passport kiosk told us, "but you are stateless, you will stay here."

"We are only passing through," I kept saying. I showed him our airline tickets to Los Angeles and our immigration papers to the States. Eventually the immigration officer stamped the *parwanat eboor* (the Iranian laissez-passer) and allowed us to stay in London for three days.

Unlike in Holland, the British made it clear that they did not want refugees like us. That left a bad taste in our mouths. However, we tried to make the most of our time there. We stayed at the home of Yvette's cousin Jack, and we toured the city and met with friends from school who had settled in London.

Our plane to Los Angeles took off around midnight on Saturday, April 29, 1972. It was a DC-8, a very long, narrow-body plane. The flight was rough; it felt like the plane wobbled up and down and sideways. But nothing could dampen our spirits. We were on our way to Los Angeles. Yvette and I were about to start a new life and have a chance to achieve our dreams. Suddenly, I felt anxious, and I could not stop the racing thoughts in my mind. *Are my expectations too high?* I put my hand on my pocket. *This is all we have in this world, just short of $2,000. Are our dreams realistic?*

Our first stop in the States shortly after midnight was at Bangor, Maine. At the passport kiosk we were asked to step aside. A short, heavyset man with thin blond hair and blue eyes came toward us a few minutes later. He wore a khaki uniform with a badge and introduced himself as the immigration officer. The three of us walked through the terminal, a big hangar, to a small makeshift office where the officer asked us to sit across the desk from him. He opened the big envelope we got at the American consulate in Rotterdam and studied the paperwork that came inside. Then he opened a smaller envelope and pulled out our green cards, checked them, and handed them to us.

"Welcome to the United States, Mr. and Mrs. Dabby," he said as he stood up and extended his hand to shake ours. "Don't forget to set your watches, we just changed to daylight saving time." It was 2:30 a.m.

No words can describe how we felt. The immigration officer made us feel very welcome at our new home. I called Charles before boarding the plane to Los Angeles. "We are here in the U.S.," I said, my voice trembling with excitement.

"I can't wait to see you," Charles said.

We arrived in Los Angeles early in the morning. Charles was not at the terminal or on the sidewalk. I called him collect from a public phone. The phone rang and rang, and I almost gave up when Charles finally picked up.

"I was so excited I could not sleep all night. I must have dozed off," Charles said. "I am sorry I am not there. Just take a cab to my apartment."

The cab drove on La Cienega Boulevard, and all we could see was open land, oil rigs, one-story buildings, and lots of big billboards. *Where are the high-rises? This is not the America we expected.* Yvette and I looked at each other with wonderment.

Charles was waiting in the lobby of his building on Burton Way. We were all happy and excited, and we hugged and hugged.

"I can't believe it, you are finally here," Charles said as he took the suitcase from Yvette and headed to the elevator. We stood inside the elevator looking at each other. After a while we realized the elevator had not moved because no one had pressed the button!

During the few quiet moments in the elevator, I thought that it was time to start our life.

"We found our new home. We are not moving again," I told Yvette.

THE BEGINNING

Me, Charles, and Yvette, 1991.

Los Angeles, 2009. Top row, left to right: Berta,
Aharon, Chas, Tikva, and Edmund.
Seated: Teresa and Charles.

Me, Yvette, Teresa, and Charles, 2016.

Cousins in Los Angeles, 2009. Left to right: Jack, Yoland, Lydia, Irit, Kathy, Uriel, Naomi, Nava, Sabrina, and Joe.

Charles and me, 2017.

Berta, me, and Tikva, 2018.

Los Angeles, 2019. Top row, left to right: Lisa, Yvette, me, Jack, Irit, Joe, Chas, Naomi, and Ethan. Bottom row: Kathy, Eva, Lydia, Teresa, Sami, Yoland, and Madeline.

*Left to right: Albert, Rosy, me, Yvette, Victoria
(Yvette's aunt), and Ezra.*

*Rachel with Ron and Monica Drori and family.
Left to right: Ron Drori, Eliahu , Miryam, Rachel,
Dvorah, Naomi, Monica, and Ovadia.*

From a Family of Two
to a Family of Twelve

Yvette started preparing and cooking for Rosh Hashanah (New Year) dinner one week in advance. On the day of September 29, 2019, tables and chairs were brought in from the storage shack in our backyard and set up in the family room as one long table with twenty-two chairs around it.

Dishes for *brachot* were placed on the table. Pots simmered on the cooktop. Small dishes with nuts, dates, and dried fruits were laid on the coffee table in the living room. Bottles of wine were opened, and wine glasses sat waiting next to them. Flowers adorned the living and family rooms. The wonderful aroma of flowers mixed with that of cooking permeated the house.

The doorbell announced our first guests. "Oh my God, I have to change," Yvette said as she pulled her apron off and ran to the bedroom.

The first to arrive was Lisa, our middle daughter, and her family. Lisa, then forty-one, slim and tall with long black hair,

Rosh Hashanah dinner table.

stood at the door with a bunch of red roses in her hands. Before she and her husband, Brian, stepped into the house, her eldest, ten-year-old Ethan, sneaked in, followed by his two siblings.

"Nana, Nana, look what Zachary, Maddie, and I made for you!"

The three kids were so different. Ethan had his father's face and curly red hair. Zachary had Lisa's face and straight blond hair, and Maddie had a little bit of both parents' features. Yvette hugged the three grandchildren and admired the work of art they had made for her.

Lisa and Brian, with Ethan, Zachary, and Madeline.

"I like this house much more than the one on North Rodeo Drive. This area is so much quieter and the neighbors are so much nicer," Lisa said.

"Why don't you move next to us?" I asked.

"Ask Brian. He thinks the world ends east of the 405 freeway," Lisa said. "He will not move far from his parents in Santa Monica, and we love the house you found for us in Brentwood."

"Were you and your sisters born on North Rodeo Drive?" Brian asked.

"No," Lisa answered, "we were all born on Linnington Ave. Later Dad built the Rodeo house."

"Baba, look who is here." Nadine, my youngest daughter, at thirty-eight, was at the door carrying her one-year-old, Victoria, and holding the hand of her three-year-old, Joel. Peter, her husband, followed her with a bottle of wine.

Nadine and Peter, with Joel and Victoria.

"When did you get in town?" I asked as I hugged Joel.

"Around noon," Nadine said. "The drive from Palo Alto took six hours today." Nadine, with a PhD in computation and neural systems from Caltech, worked in innovation at Intel near Palo Alto, where she and her family lived.

"Don't close the door," Nadine said. "Teresa is here."

Teresa, my late brother Charles's wife, walked up the stairs with a bottle of wine.

"I wish Charles was here with us today," I said as I hugged her.

"It has already been one year since he passed," Teresa said. "Can you believe how time flies?" Teresa and Charles were married for more than twenty years.

"Time really flies. It is already forty-seven years since Charles brought us to Los Angeles," I said, nodding my head. "Did you talk to Chas and Trina?" I asked.

Rosy and Mark.

"Yes, they should be here any minute. I hear Chas is playing golf now."

"Yes, he played with me at my club last week, and he is good," I said. I have been playing golf since 1992.

Chas, Charles's son, and his wife, Trina, walked in. The kids ran and jumped all over Chas, who started making faces and gestures to scare them.

"Lisa, can you text Naomi and ask for her ETA?" Yvette asked.

The doorbell rang, and Albert pushed the door open. "*Shana Tova* [Happy New Year], everyone."

His wife, Rosy (Yvette's sister), followed him carrying a dish. "Jaimie and Joey and the kids will be here soon. Marc promised to come too," Rosy announced with a smile. "Ezra will also come sometime tonight!"

Jaimie and Marc are Rosy and Albert's children who were

Nadine, Lisa, and Naomi.

both born in Holland before the family moved to Los Angeles in 1989. Jaimie and her husband, Joey, have two children, Gabriel and Sophia. Ezra is Yvette's brother, who studied architecture and worked in Holland before moving to Los Angeles to be close to family. He has two sons who lived with their mother in Israel.

"Hi, everyone," Naomi walked in with seven light balloons. "Where are the kids?"

Naomi, my eldest daughter at forty-five, has big brown eyes and shoulder-length black hair. "I invited two friends. Can we wait a few minutes?" she asked.

"Al isn't here yet," Nadine said. Al, her professor from Caltech, had been coming to our holiday dinners for the last two years. Yvette ran to add three chairs at the table for the guests. Naomi was having a blast, surrounded by the kids, who were enthralled by the sight of the light balloons.

Jaimie and Joey.

Jaimie, Joey, and their children were the next group to arrive. Joey handed me a small bottle. "This is our latest product—marijuana-infused drink!" I opened the bottle and took a big sip.

"Not too much, Uncle Joe," Jaimie warned me. "This stuff really works."

We sat in the living room, and Peter started to play the piano.

"Dad," Lisa said, "I took the kids to the dentist the other day, and Ethan loved the dentist's office building on Beverly Drive." Ethan nodded.

"Baba Joe, Mom told me that you and Nana developed that building. I love it," Ethan said.

"I love it, too, and one day I will show you a few more of our projects," I said.

I turned to Albert, who had just come from the synagogue. "Albert, how was the service?"

"The service was wonderful," Albert said. "At least thirty people were in attendance."

Lisa, me, Yvette, Naomi, and Nadine.

Yvette and I found Kahal Joseph in 1972 and never left it. The synagogue was started by a small, diverse community whose members were of Iraqi origin but had come to Los Angeles from India, Burma, Singapore, and other Asian countries. The community, at least three generations removed from the old country, kept their customs and traditions intact. They spoke Judeo-Arabic like us, and their prayers and melodies were the same as the ones we grew up with. When I took Dad to a Shabbat service there, he got very emotional and started crying.

Yvette and I have become very involved in Kahal Joseph and have been working hard to keep the synagogue alive and to perpetuate the Baghdadi customs and traditions for our children and grandchildren. We helped to plan and construct the current synagogue building in West Los Angeles and served on its board for years both as directors and as presidents.

The grandkids: Madeline, Joel, Victoria, Ethan, and Zachary.

When everyone had finally arrived, we moved to the family room and sat around the long table.

"*Shana Tova.*" I looked at the kids who were very loud. "Ethan, quiet please." I raised my voice to be heard. "Let's all give Yvette a hand for this beautiful evening." Everyone applauded. I recited the *kiddush* (holy day blessing) and asked the children to help me with the *hamotzi* (blessing on the bread). The kids came next to me and recited the blessing with me. I proceeded to cut the challah. When one of the kids started crying, the long sharp bread knife slipped in my hand and cut my left forefinger. Blood shot out. Naomi and Lisa both jumped and ran to check my cut.

"Oh my God, the cut is too deep, you will need stitches," Naomi said.

"I will run home for my medical bag," Lisa said.

"Whoa, doctors, I don't need anything, just a Band-Aid. Let's sit down and eat," I said to Naomi and Lisa, both ER physicians.

"I warned you, Uncle Joe," Jaimie said. "That drink is really effective."

Everyone was laughing, including the kids, who started to sing, led by Chas, "Baba is high, Baba is high!"

"It's not the drink." Everyone shook their heads; I was not convincing. "Come on, let's have dinner. I am okay."

Lisa wrapped my finger with a gauze bandage. "Your cut is too deep, you need at least six stitches."

Everyone took part in saying the Rosh Hashanah *brachot* (blessings).

"I am very impressed. Where did you girls learn Hebrew?" Al asked.

"We went to Hillel Hebrew Academy for elementary school," Lisa said.

"You know, Al, Dad planned and built the new school building," Nadine said.

"In the other room I saw the many awards and the two proclamations honoring your parents," Al said. "You girls must be very proud."

"We certainly are," Lisa answered.

The proclamations Al referred to were from the cities of Los Angeles and Beverly Hills recognizing Yvette's and my services to the community. In addition, the City of Beverly Hills named January 14, 1990, "Yvette and Joseph Dabby Day" in our honor.

During dinner everyone talked. It was heartwarming for me to look around the table and see how our family has grown.

Our three daughters, all born in Los Angeles, made us proud.

"I miss Savtah's [Grandma's] *pacha*," Nadine said.

"You saw your grandparents?" asked Joey.

"Of course," Nadine replied. "Savtah and Baba used to live with us."

Lisa nodded in agreement. "We were so fortunate—they moved here when I was born," she said.

My parents joined us in 1979, a few years after we settled in Los Angeles, and stayed with us until they passed, Dad in 1989 and Mom in 1990.

"Grandma Farha, Mom's mother, and her sister Vicky also moved here to be with us," Naomi chimed in. "We are blessed to have known our grandparents."

After dinner Lisa ran to her home in Brentwood and brought her medical bag.

"I will do the stitches," Naomi said, taking the medical bag from Lisa.

I watched Naomi stitching the cut in my finger meticulously. My hand looked so old, with blue veins bulging through thin, wrinkled skin and crooked fingers with swollen joints. I recalled my young hands, their thick, tight skin with the veins hardly showing and the fingers straight and thin. I shook my head in denial.

"I am almost done," Naomi said. "Are you okay?"

"Yes," I said. "I was just wondering where the time went."

That night after everyone left, Yvette and I surveyed the messy family room.

"That was a lot of work," Yvette said, "but I loved every minute."

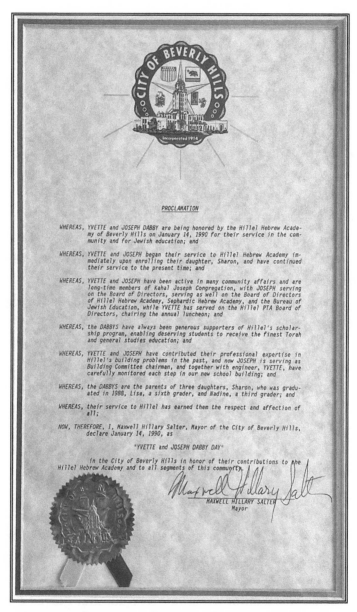

*Two awards Yvette and I received in 1990: one from the
City of Beverly Hills (above) and one from the City of
Los Angeles (opposite).*

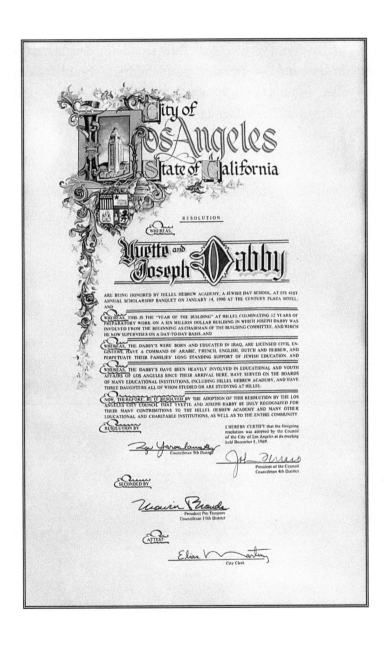

City of Los Angeles
State of California

RESOLUTION

WHEREAS,

Yvette and Joseph Dabby

ARE BEING HONORED BY HILLEL HEBREW ACADEMY, A JEWISH DAY SCHOOL, AT ITS 41ST
ANNUAL SCHOLARSHIP BANQUET ON JANUARY 14, 1990 AT THE CENTURY PLAZA HOTEL;
AND

WHEREAS, THIS IS THE "YEAR OF THE BUILDING" AT HILLEL CULMINATING 12 YEARS OF
PREPARATORY WORK ON A SIX MILLION DOLLAR BUILDING IN WHICH JOSEPH DABBY WAS
INVOLVED FROM THE BEGINNING AS CHAIRMAN OF THE BUILDING COMMITTEE, AND WHICH
HE NOW SUPERVISES ON A DAY-TO-DAY BASIS; AND

WHEREAS, THE DABBY'S WERE BORN AND EDUCATED IN IRAQ, ARE LICENSED CIVIL EN-
GINEERS, HAVE A COMMAND OF ARABIC, FRENCH, ENGLISH, DUTCH AND HEBREW, AND
PERPETUATE THEIR FAMILIES' LONG STANDING SUPPORT OF JEWISH EDUCATION; AND

WHEREAS, THE DABBY'S HAVE BEEN HEAVILY INVOLVED IN EDUCATIONAL AND YOUTH
AFFAIRS OF LOS ANGELES SINCE THEIR ARRIVAL HERE, HAVE SERVED ON THE BOARDS
OF MANY EDUCATIONAL INSTITUTIONS, INCLUDING HILLEL HEBREW ACADEMY, AND HAVE
THREE DAUGHTERS ALL OF WHOM STUDIED OR ARE STUDYING AT HILLEL;

NOW, THEREFORE, BE IT RESOLVED BY THE ADOPTION OF THIS RESOLUTION BY THE LOS
ANGELES CITY COUNCIL THAT YVETTE AND JOSEPH DABBY BE DULY RECOGNIZED FOR
THEIR MANY CONTRIBUTIONS TO THE HILLEL HEBREW ACADEMY AND MANY OTHER
EDUCATIONAL AND CHARITABLE INSTITUTIONS, AS WELL AS TO THE ENTIRE COMMUNITY

RESOLUTION BY

Zev Yaroslavsky
Councilman 5th District

I HEREBY CERTIFY that the foregoing
resolution was adopted by the Council
of the City of Los Angeles at its meeting
held December 5, 1989.

President of the Council
Councilman 4th District

SECONDED BY

Marvin Braude
President Pro Tempore
Councilman 11th District

ATTEST

Elias Martinez
City Clerk

"We have been very blessed—three wonderful daughters, two sons-in-law, and five amazing grandchildren," I said, looking at Yvette. "From a family of two to a family of twelve, we have come a long way from Baghdad."

Yvette and me on our fifty-first wedding anniversary.

APPENDIX

A Quick History of Iraq and Iraqi Jews

The Iraqi Jews, known as the Babylonian or Mizrahi Jews, are one of the oldest Jewish communities in the world. Their history is documented back to 721 BCE, when Jews were brought to what is today Iraq by the Assyrians following their conquest of the Northern Kingdom of Israel.

In 597 BCE, during the Babylonian rule, came the biggest influx of Jews into what is now Iraq. Nebuchadnezzar II, king of Babylon, conquered the Southern Kingdom of Israel (Judah) and partially destroyed Jerusalem and the Holy Temple. He brought back to Babylon the king of Judah, his court, and thousands of men as slaves.

In 586 BCE, the Judeans revolted. This time Nebuchadnezzar destroyed Jerusalem and the Temple and deported thousands more Jews as slaves to Babylon. This was followed by a third captivity and influx in the year 581 BCE.

Psalm 137:1–9 paints a clear picture of the exiles' experience in Babylonia after the destruction of Jerusalem and the Temple:

By the rivers of Babylon we sat and wept
when we remembered Zion.
There on the poplars
we hung our harps,
for there our captors asked us for songs,
our tormentors demanded songs of joy;
they said, "Sing us one of the songs of Zion!"

How can we sing the songs of the Lord
while in a foreign land?
If I forget you, Jerusalem,
may my right hand forget its skill.
May my tongue cling to the roof of my mouth
if I do not remember you,
if I do not consider Jerusalem
my highest joy.

Remember, Lord, what the Edomites did
on the day Jerusalem fell.
"Tear it down," they cried,
"tear it down to its foundations!"
Daughter Babylon, doomed to destruction,
happy is the one who repays you
according to what you have done to us.
Happy is the one who seizes your infants
and dashes them against the rocks.

The Jewish captives' accomplishments were remarkable. It was in Babylonia where Ezra the Scribe started the Pharisaic movement (Rabbinic Judaism), and Hillel established the Mishnah (the oral law). Several yeshivot (academies) were built in Iraq, such as Nehardea and Pumbedita, and by the year 500 CE the Talmud Babli (Babylonian Talmud) was completed. The Talmud is a collection of the writings of rabbis dating from the Common Era through the fifth century. It is the basis for all codes of Jewish law and is still in use by Jews all over the world today.

In 539 BCE Babylon was conquered by the Persians. Cyrus the Great permitted the Jews to return to their native land and rebuild the Temple. The majority, however, remained in Babylonia and thrived in relative independence and religious freedom.

The Jewish population in Iraq remained small but lasted through the many empires that passed through the area: the Greeks (Alexander the Great), the Romans, the Persians, the Arab Caliphate that came from Syria, and the Abbasid Caliphate that ruled the area from 750 CE to 1258 CE.

The city of Baghdad, founded in 762 CE, became the capital of the Abbasid Caliphate and the center of learning for the entire Muslim world. Under Islam, the Jews paid jizya (poll tax) to ensure their freedom of religion and safety. Jews began to speak in Arabic instead of Aramaic and wrote their work in Hebrew and in Arabic in Hebrew script.

In 1258 the Mongols invaded the region, which led to its decline. They were followed by the Jalayirids (Persian Mongols) and the Timurid Dynasty (Turco Mongols) in the fourteenth century. In 1532 the Ottoman Turks, after a long struggle, conquered Baghdad and the Tigris and Euphrates Valley. The region remained part of the vast Ottoman Empire until the end of World War I in 1918.

The Ottoman Empire reformed its laws in the mid-nineteenth century and allowed minorities such as Jews to participate in the Ottoman government. Jews were legal advisers and councilors to governors. In 1877 Menahem Saleh Efendi Daniel became a member of the Ottoman parliament representing Baghdad. In 1908, after the Young Turk Revolution, Sassoon Efendi Heskell was elected to the Ottoman parliament for Baghdad and was returned to this seat twice more before the dissolution of the Ottoman Empire in 1918.

As the Turkish rule deteriorated, the situation of the Jews worsened, but the population continued to grow. In 1884 there were thirty thousand Jews in Baghdad, and by 1900 there were fifty thousand. The community produced great rabbis, such as Yosef Hayyim ben Eliahu Mazal-Tov, also known as the Ben Ish Hai (1834–1909), who was best known for his work on the *Halakha*, followed by the Jews everywhere. Jews served in the Ottoman army and fought in Turkish units or were doctors and translators during World War I.

Soon after their defeat in WWI, the Ottomans threw the blame on the Jews and accused them of shirking their duty in the war effort. Some were executed; many others saw their properties confiscated.

In 1919 Britain and France divided the Middle East into today's countries. Iraq was established as a kingdom following the British system of government and placed under the British Mandate. King Faisal I, a descendant of the prophet Muhammad, was installed by the British as the first king of the Hashemite

Kingdom that ruled Iraq until 1958. Sunni Muslims, a minority of the population, were chosen by the British to dominate the political life.

The Jews flourished during the British Mandate (1920–1932). There were around 250,000 Jews in the country; they constituted 15 percent of the population of Iraq and 25 percent of the population of Baghdad. Iraqi Jews were international because of their connections to the small Jewish communities that emigrated during the Ottoman rule to Britain, India, and Shanghai. They were multilingual, and their educational network that had started in the 1850s was large and influential.

The British saw all of that and invited Jews to participate in building the newborn country. The Jews were essential to the development of Iraq's economic, judicial, and postal systems. Iraqi music and songs were shaped and developed by Jewish musicians and artists. Jewish men served in the Iraqi parliament and held top positions in most governmental offices. Iraq's first minister of finance was a Jew, Sir Sassoon Heskell. He is well known for having the British agree to pay for Iraqi oil in gold and not in British currency. This was the best of times for Iraqi Jewry.

With the death of King Faisal I and the introduction of Nazi propaganda by King Ghazi (1933–1939), things changed. On August 27, 1934, many Jews were dismissed from public service, and quotas were set up in colleges and universities. The teaching of Jewish history and the Hebrew language in Jewish schools was banned. Following Rashid Ali al-Gaylani's pro-Axis coup in 1941, the Farhud ("violent dispossession") pogrom broke out in Baghdad, during which approximately 180 Jews were murdered and up to 1,000 injured; damages to property were estimated at $3 million.

Following the birth of the State of Israel in 1948, Zionism was declared a capital crime in Iraqi law. Jews were not allowed to serve in the Iraqi army anymore. Hundreds of Jews were accused of Zionism or Communism and were imprisoned, and many of them were accused of spying for Israel and hanged in public. Jews were forbidden from dealing with banks, and their import and export licenses were revoked. They were dismissed from the railways, the post office, financial institutions, and all governmental offices.

In July of 1948 Shafiq Ades, a wealthy and prominent Jew, was accused of being a Zionist and a Communist. Ades owned the Ford dealership in Basra. He was accused of sending cars to Israel and donating money to the Communist Party. He was hanged in public, and all his assets were confiscated. No one believed that this could happen to someone so prominent, someone who befriended top government officials and dined with the king and the regent.

The Jews started to flee the country by crossing the border into Iran. To stop the illegal emigration and the loss of the educated, the Iraqi government implemented the Denaturalization Act in 1950. Jews would be allowed to emigrate to Israel if they renounced their Iraqi citizenship. In what was later known as the Big Aliyah, 120,000 Iraqi Jews left for Israel in 1951 and 1952, leaving all of their possessions behind.

The emigration of the Jews was stopped in 1952. New economic restrictions were imposed on those who remained in the country. Big companies were ordered to lay off their Jewish employees, and Jewish kids were not allowed to attend public schools. Travel abroad was restricted. Within the country, movement and activities of the Jews were restricted. As a result, the community was isolated, and it became one large, tightly knit family. Gatherings to celebrate or to mourn were held quietly and in low profile, and outside their homes, everyone spoke in the Muslim dialect to blend in with the population.

After the Big Aliyah, the Jewish community in Iraq numbered around twenty-five thousand and lived mostly in Baghdad. That number dwindled to a single digit in the next twenty-five years. Only three synagogues remained operational in 1960 (out of sixty in 1950), and life for the Jews was anything but normal.

The years that followed the Six-Day War in 1967 were even more difficult. Phone service in Jewish homes and businesses was disconnected. The licenses of Jewish merchants were canceled. Jewish bank accounts were frozen. Companies and businesses were told to dismiss Jewish employees. Jewish men were imprisoned and tortured, and bribes were demanded to release them. A new law allowed the authorities to arrest Jews and keep them in prison indefinitely without a reason or trial. Forty-five well-known Jewish men from all walks of life were taken to the central prison in Al-Adhamiyah, where they were held for around two years, no reason given. In spite of its precarious existence, the community tried to maintain its optimism and led as normal a life as was possible.

Rabbi Sasson Khadouri was the chief rabbi of the community. The Jewish Community Office handled all the Jewish affairs—it issued birth, marriage, and death certificates; managed the synagogues, schools, and the Jewish cemetery; and took care of the poor. Synagogues were supported by funds raised from the community and from trusts established by philanthropists for that purpose. Community schools were free for those who could not afford them.

On July 14, 1958, Abd al-Karim Qasim staged a military coup that did away with the monarchy, and Iraq became a republic. During Qasim's rule (1958–1963), the Jews were allowed more freedom and experienced less discrimination and were allowed to leave the country. That ended when he was killed and the Ba'athists took over. Over the next decade, Iraq saw four coups d'état. In the mid-1960s the Iraqi government implemented a policy of systematic discrimination. Jews were not allowed to leave the country and had to carry a yellow identity card with the word *Moussawi* (follower of Moses) written in red.

In 1969, after a series of mock trials, fifty-one Jews were hanged in public squares of Iraqi cities. Top military men and politicians were accused of associating with the Jews and were executed along with the Jews as spies. Despite the danger to their lives and their families, Jews continued to escape the country to Iran with the help of the Kurds, and their number dwindled to four hundred in the mid-1970s and to around forty by the time Iraq was freed of Saddam Hussein's rule in 2003.

Today only four or five known Jews live in Iraq.

Iraq has been cleansed of the Jews who lived there for 2,700 years.

About The Author

Joseph H. Dabby was born in Baghdad, Iraq, in 1946 to a middle-class Jewish family. Growing up as a Jew in Iraq after World War II and during the birth and growth of the State of Israel was not a pleasant experience, to say the least. Dabby was imprisoned twice before he and his wife, Yvette, both civil engineers, escaped from Iraq in 1971, emigrated to the United States, and made Los Angeles their new home. Since their arrival in Los Angeles, the Dabbys have been very active in Jewish education, and as leaders of their small community of Jews of Iraqi origin, they continue their work to perpetuate their traditions and customs. Yvette and Joseph have three daughters, Naomi, Lisa, and Nadine, who urged their father to write this story, so that their children and grandchildren can learn where they came from and appreciate what they have.

Ingram Content Group UK Ltd.
Milton Keynes UK
UKHW040859190323
418701UK00003B/29/J